Deliberate Self-Harm in Substance Abuse Population

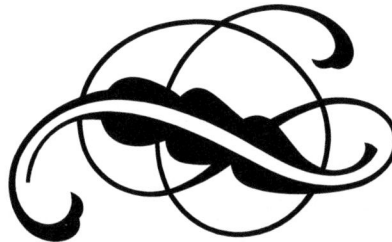

Dr Samia Abul

Psychiatrist

To order additional copies of this book, contact:
Xlibris LLC
0-800-056-3182
www.xlibrispublishing.co.uk
Orders@ Xlibrispublishing.co.uk

Dedication

To the source of:
My Happiness,
My Security,
My Power,
My Love;
My precious mother.

Foreword

Reading this book has gained to my knowledge in a tremendous way. It has opened my eyes to something I hadn't known it exists in our world. It has shown me a whole other issue that I had not taken into consideration and it is quiet a sensitive one as a matter of fact.

The way it is written had made it so easy for a person, a reader to understand each aspect of it and differentiate it from other health problems of the same characteristic. I think people would benefit from this book in a remarkable way, as it may also help them in their lives.

Seeing the people around them, they may not know that they have this problem and this book would help them help their families and loved ones. This would be a benefit amongst many others to the readers of this book. Just gaining the insight would be a huge advantage.

I for one found the topic very interesting and craved reading more and more, didn't really know why myself but I just kept it close to my eyes. In addition, this book would really be a great call for awareness for this mental illness, and people would know how to deal with people having this illness and not jump to conclusions.

A book like this cannot be useless and as Philosopher Henry David Thoreau said "Read the best books first, or you may not have a chance to read them at all", this is one of those books that need to be read.

Aisha Al Sahlawi

Preface

Deliberate Self-Harm (DSH) in Substance Abuse Population provides an in-depth look at the history of deliberate self-harm in clients attending two London-based Drug Treatment and Testing Orders (DTTO) Services. This book was compiled in requirement for degree of Master of Science in Clinical and Public Health Aspects of Addiction at present of National Addiction Centre-Institute of Psychiatry King's College-University of London.

Deliberate self-harm in substance abuse population, as a serious behaviour, has been cold-shouldered by many for a long time. There are various reasons for such an attitude. But the most common exhibition is unfamiliarity with the subject.

This book aims to present a brief yet comprehensive account of deliberate self-harm in substance abuse population and their allied aspects. While striving to make the book enjoyable, easy to follow, as well as useful, an attempt has been made to bring attention to an important issue by putting scientific knowledge in a simple, systematic, and illustrative way. As this book is very readable, it is also good teaching, and will find favour with professionals and those interested in DSH.

The author is grateful to the many unsung heroes who helped me move the book to completion. Without their efforts, this book would not have happened.

Dr Samia Abul
Dubai 2014

Acknowledgement

Collaborative effects of many individuals made this book possible. Special thanks are due to Dr Jane Marshall for her helpful discussions, comments, and corrections; Dr Emily Finch, consultant psychiatrist in charge of the Croydon & Lambeth, Southwark and Lewisham (LSL) DTTO, for her permission to use the LSL DTTO project as research setting and for her continuous support; Dr Mariam Saeed for her valuable assistance and encouragement; and Dr Kim Wolff for her kind advice.

I am grateful to the senior probation officers and in charge nurses and the teams of both Croydon and LSL DTTO services and the statistical team at the Institute of Psychiatry, especially Miss Nora Donaldson for her help in the statistical analysis.

All participants deserve special thanks. Finally, sincere thanks to my husband, Ahmad Rafi, and my son, Omar Ahmad Rafi, for their love and support during the writing and revision of this book.

Contents

Appendixes

Tables

Table 1. Reasons, length of current DTTO, and length of previous time in prison of Croydon and LSL offenders.

Table 2. Detailed data about consumption of alcohol in DSH and non-DSH.

Table 3. Detailed data about use of heroin in DSH and non-DSH.

Table 4. Detailed data about use of cocaine/crack in DSH and non-DSH.

Table 5. Detailed data about use of cannabis in DSH and non-DSH.

Table 6. Detailed data about use of benzodiazepines in DSH and non-DSH.

Table 7. Detailed data about use of other substances in DSH and non-DSH.

Table 8. Details of preferred substance use in DSH and non-DSH.

Table 9. Relationship between DSH and non-DSH and a preferred substance use.

Table 10. Relationship between DSH and non-DSH and a preferred substance use (logistic regression).

Table 11. History of DSH of the clients attending the Croydon and LSL DTTO Services.

Table 12. Suicidal thoughts and suicidal acts.

Table 13. Relationship of heroin and alcohol users in DSH and non-DSH group.

Figures

Figure 1. Different methods of DSH reported by clients attending the Croydon and LSL DTTO services.

Figure 2. Different feelings experienced by clients before the episode of DSH.

Figure 3. Different feelings experienced by the clients after the episode of DSH.

Figure 4. Factors perceived to have provoked the episode of DSH.

2. Abstract

The links between substance misuse, deliberate self-harm, and crime have been well described in the literature. Treatment of drug misuse ranges from brief interventions by the primary health care team (PHCT) through to intensive services delivered in a controlled medical or criminal justice environment. Current treatment services are devised along a four-tier structure with tier I being predominantly identification and referral services (includes primary health care teams, arrest referral schemes, youth offender teams, and drug treatment and testing orders).

This study *aims* to describe the socio-demographic characteristics of clients who have a history of deliberate self-harm – attending a tier I scheme at Croydon & Lambeth, Southwark and Lewisham (LSL) Drug Treatment and Testing Orders Services (DTTO) – and to illustrate the correlation between deliberate self-harm and substance misuse in this client group. In addition, the study will explore the co-morbidity of deliberate self-harm with *depression* or *impulsivity* in this client group. Sixty consecutive clients attending the Croydon and LSL DTTO Services were recruited and assessed for deliberate self-harm. A self-report semi-structured questionnaire, in three parts, was used. In addition, two standardised questionnaires, The Beck Depression Inventory Scale (BDI) and the Barratt Impulsiveness Scale (BIS-11), were used. The *result* showed that the study group (n=60) was predominantly male (Male 53: Female 7), unemployed, white British and with no qualifications. The mean age was 33.9 years (+/-7.2). The majority of the clients were referred to the DTTO service for shoplifting. This study revealed that the following substances (in descending order) were used: cocaine/crack (93%), heroin (83%), cannabis (82%), alcohol (73%), benzodiazepines (40%), and other substances (18%). Of those using cocaine and heroin, 22% and 33% respectively were injecting. Of the sixty clients, thirty-nine (65%) had a history of DSH, with the mean age of the first episode of DSH being 23 years (+/-6.5). *Cutting* and *overdosing* were the most common methods of DSH, occurring in 54% and 51% of the sample respectively. Head banging (15%), picking unhealed wounds (13%) and other methods (10%) were also described by the sample. The most common feeling experienced before these episodes of DSH was 'emotional pain' (described by 64% of the sample). 'Regretfulness' was the common feeling experience after an episode of DSH (in 41% of the sample). Alcohol and drugs were frequently implicated in the episodes and were perceived to have aggravated the DSH episodes in 80% of the sample. There was no association between DSH and the type of substance used, age at first use and route of administration. Heroin was the preferred substance in the DSH group, and this association reached significance (p=0.025). Heroin users with a history of DSH were nine times more likely to use alcohol than their heroin using non-DSH counterparts. Almost half of the DSH sample had previously made a suicide attempt and 82% had a past history of a traumatic experience. There were no statistical correlations between DSH and measures of impulsivity and depression. However more subjects with a history of DSH had scores in the severe impulsive category compared with the non-DSH group (19 vs 7; NS). In *summary* this pilot study of DSH in a DTTO sample is limited by the small sample size. However, very little research has been carried out in the DTTO setting and these findings point to themes that should be tested in larger samples. No significant predictors for DSH were found with respect to socio-demographic factors, type and route of substance use, and measures of depression and impulsivity. The DTTO clients with a history of DSH were significantly more likely to prefer heroin than those without such a DSH history. Furthermore the heroin using DSH group was nine times more likely to use alcohol than their heroin using non-DSH counterparts. There was also a trend for the DSH group to have higher impulsivity scores, but this did not reach significance.

3. Introduction

Deliberate self-harm (DSH) has become a serious public and major health problem, which has increased in size during the last fifty years. The real number of persons engaging in any form of DSH is unknown; nonetheless, a reasonable estimate is that rates are around 400 per 100,000 populations per annum – probably much greater than the figures that are presently available, because in many cases, DSH instances are not recorded as such, while for most DSH, no contact is established with services (Hawton et al., 1997).

The limited accuracy and reliability of DSH statistics are, in part, attributable to the lack of a commonly accepted and applied definition of DSH. In addition to variability in the criteria for classification of DSH as an intention for death, personal bias, incomplete information, cultural resistance, and pressure of the family and community probably contribute to a marked under-reporting of DSH (Hawton et al., 1997).

3.1 Definition of Deliberate Self-Harm

Other terms can be used to describe deliberate self-harm including deliberate self poisoning, self-inflicted violence, self-cutting, self-injury, self-abuse, self-mutilation, attempted suicide or parasuicide (Favazza & Conterio, 1988). Favazza and Conterio (1988) consider the behaviour to be a deliberate destruction or alteration of body tissue without conscious suicidal intent.

Solomon and Farrand (1996) stated that DSH is the act of attempting to alter a mood state by inflicting physical harm serious enough to cause tissue damage to one's own body. The act is not a conscious attempt at suicide. It is often described as a maladaptive behaviour symptomatic of disturbance and dysfunction.

Anderson (1999) described DSH as an act which resembles suicide and which may be fatal, but the person intends to live rather than die. However, Boyce et al. (2001) stated that the term DSH includes all acts, whether they have the purpose of attempting to kill oneself (attempting suicide) or other purpose, such as help seeking, tension release, or expressing inner anger (parasuicide). DSH was defined by Dhossche et al. (2000) as any act resulting in physical harm requiring acute medical attention. DSH is defined as purposeful and intentional self-harm, while other cases are categorised as accidental self-harm. Winchel (1991) stated that DSH is a commission of deliberate harm to one's own body without the aid of other person, and the injury is severe enough for tissue damage (such as scarring) to result. Acts that are committed with conscious suicidal intent or are associated with sexual arousal are excluded. DSH is an act that is usually aimed at bringing about change which the subject desired via the actual or expected consequences of the DSH, or escaping an intolerable situation (O'Connor et al., 2000). Favazza and Rosenthal (1993) suggest defining DSH as a disease and not merely a symptom. They created a diagnostic category called Repetitive Self-Harm Syndrome. The diagnostic criteria for Repetitive Self-Harm Syndrome include preoccupation with physically harming oneself; repeated failure to resist impulses to destroy or alter one's body tissue; increasing tension right before, and a sense of relief after self-harm; no association between suicidal intent and the act of self-harm; and not a response to mental retardation, delusion, hallucination.

DSH is an intentional, self-inflicted act commonly affected by physical means (drug overdose or poisoning). It is the act of injuring oneself to help to cope with and block out and release built-up feelings and emotions. It describes any non-fatal deliberate act of self-harm. It is away to deal with extreme emotional distress, a way to survive. It's anything that causes you harm and pain (Hawton et al., 2002).

3.2 Demographic Characteristics of Deliberate Self-Harm

Deliberate self-harm is a significant and costly health problem, and it is increasing, particularly among younger ages (O'Sullivan et al., 1999). Data from Oxford, UK, showed an increase of approximately 28% in the numbers of DSH patients of both sexes between the periods 1985–1986 and 1994–1995, with an increase of approximately 50% of repeated DSH in both sexes (Hawton et al., 1997). Characteristics of

DSH among alcohol abusers include being male, of older age, divorced, separated or widowed, living alone, and being unemployed (Haw et al., 2001).

A recent study by Powis et al. (1999) showed that instances of overdosing are common (38%), and over 80% of the subjects who had overdosed had done so in presence of someone else, but only 27% reported that ambulances were called. Women were more likely to overdose than men, and alcohol and polydrug use were associated with overdosing (Powis et al., 1999). DSH is one of the most common reasons for emergency hospital admission in Great Britain (Gunnell et al., 2002); 90% cases referred to general hospitals in the United Kingdom involve self-poisoning, especially with paracetamol (Hawton et al., 1997). Although there were once between two or three times as many episodes in females (Holdsworth et al., 2001; Morgan & Coleman, 2000; Townsend et al., 2001; Zaidan et al., 2002), the sex-specific rates have steadily drawn closer together. DSH is now only slightly more common among women than men; some general hospitals now deal with more referrals of men than women (House et al., 1992). The mean age of DSH population is in the early thirties for both sexes, the peak age for presentation being fifteen to twenty-four years for women and twenty-five to thirty-four years for men (Charlton, 1995).

3.3 Methods of Deliberate Self-Harm

Drug overdose is the most common method of deliberate self-harm in both sexes. Self-cutting and hitting are also common, but jumping from high places or the use of firearms were less common (Michel et al., 2000). It seems there are no differences in psychopathology related to the method of DSH. However, de Moore and Robertson (1999) noticed that those who jumped were more likely to be psychotic, while those who used firearms were more likely to be male, abuse alcohol, and have a forensic history and a diagnosis of personality disorder.

Favazza (1989) separated DSH into three types:

1. Major self-mutilation (including castration of limbs, enucleating of eyes), which is rare and usually associated with psychotic states.

2. Stereotypic self-harm comprises the sort of rhythmic head-banging, seen in autistic, mentally retarded, and psychotic people.

3. Superficial or moderate self-harm, which is the most common form and includes cutting, burning, scratching, skin-picking, hair-pulling, bone-breaking, hitting, interference with wound injuries, and deliberate overdosing.

Favazza (1996) further breaks down superficial /moderate self-harm in to three types:

compulsive, episodic, and repetitive. Compulsive self-harm differs in character from the other two types and is more closely associated with obsessive compulsive disorder (OCD). Compulsive self-harm comprises hair-pulling (trichotillomania), skin-picking, and excoriation when it is done to remove perceived faults or blemishes in the skin. These acts may be part of OCD ritual involving obsessional thoughts. The person tries to relieve tension and prevent some bad thing from happening by engaging in these self-harm behaviours (Favazza, 1996).

Compulsive self-harm has a somewhat different nature and has different roots from impulsive (episodic and repetitive) types of self-harm. Both episodic and repetitive self-harm are impulsive acts, and the difference between them seems to be a matter of degree. Episodic self-harm is self-injurious behaviour engaged in every so often by people who don't think about it otherwise and don't see themselves as self-injurers. It generally is a symptom of some other psychological disorder. What begins as episodic self-harm can escalate into repetitive self-harm, which many practitioners (Favazza & Rosenthal, 1993; Kahan & Pattison, 1984; among others) believe should be classified as a separate axis I impulse-control disorder.

Repetitive self-harm is marked by a shift towards ruminating on self-injury even when not actually doing it and self-identification as a self-injury. Episodic self-harm becomes repetitive when what was formerly a symptom becomes a disease in itself. It is impulsive in nature and often becomes a reflex response to any sort of stress, positive or negative (Favazza, 1996).

3.4 Deliberate Self-Harm Co-morbid with Other Psychiatric Disorders

Individuals who exhibit DSH have been described as immature young people with unstable background and multiple social problems (Harrington, 2001). Deliberate self-harm presents as a symptom of psychopathology in a range of psychiatric conditions including schizophrenia and other psychosis (Conn & Lion, 1983). According to the Diagnostic and Statistical Manual of Mental Disorders (DSM-IIIR), impulsive, self-injury behaviour among non-psychotic, intellectually normal individuals may be diagnosed as either impulse-control disorder or 'not otherwise specified' or as a symptom of borderline personality disorder (Winchel, 1991).

DSH is associated with axis II disorders, borderline personality disorder (BPD), and antisocial personality disorder. BPD is highly associated with DSH behaviour, and this is shown in a number of studies (Boyce et al., 2001; Brown et al., 2002; Casillas, 2002; Sansone et al., 2002). Casillas (2002) documented the strong relationship between DSH and impulsivity, which plays a significant role in cluster B personality disorder and substance use disorders.

Substance abuse disorders occur more commonly in DSH groups than non-DSH groups. A report from Birmingham has confirmed that the association between alcohol-related problems and DSH remains a strong one (Merrill et al., 1992). Because of the clinical importance of the relation between substance use and DSH, the management of patients who received a diagnosis of alcohol or drug dependence at the time of psychiatric assessment for an episode of DSH was examined by Wylie et al. (1996). The result showed that alcohol was consumed in the period immediately before or during the episode of DSH in both sexes.

Another study indicated that alcohol had been taken in the six hours preceding the act of DSH. Both the chronic disruption inherent in alcohol addiction and immediate effects of alcohol intake are important in DSH and are sufficiently common to make routine search for them imperative, especially in men (Dunkel et al., 2002).

Substance abuse disorders and co-morbid depression are also associated with DSH, and this combination is associated with a high level of suicidal intention. Dhossche et al. (2000) advises any individuals presenting with DSH should be carefully assessed for co-morbidity of substance abuse. DSH is associated with drug dependence, especially intravenous use of heroin rather than oral use (Gossop et al., 1975). Another study showed the relation between DSH and heroin drug injectors (Powis et al., 1999). Manfredini et al. (1994) have showed that the highest rate found for DSH is in the early morning. Blenkiron et al. (2000) confirmed Manfredini's study and also found that the early (0300 to 1459 hours) act of DSH is associated with depressive disorder and with more suicidal ideation, while the late (1500 to 0259 hours) act of DSH was more associated with alcohol use.

Depression is very common among people with DSH tendencies. Many studies have reported significant rates of depressive illness in individuals with DSH. Suominen et al. (1996) and Haw et al. (2002) found that DSH is associated with co-morbidity with respect to depression and alcohol abuse or dependence. Co-morbidity of DSH with depression and personality disorder is also very common; co-morbidity with alcohol abuse or personality disorder and poor compliance with treatment have been shown to complicate the management in many depressed DSH patients (Haw et al., 2002).

There is a link between substance abuse and impulsivity. Brandy et al. (1998) documented that impulsive and aggressive individuals have a higher rate of substance abuse than the general population. It is, however, hard to know whether DSH is related to substance abuse or is due to other factors (e.g. concomitant antisocial personality disorder (ASPD) or aggression), Moeller et al. (2002) studied the increased impulsivity in cocaine dependent subjects and found out that increased impulsivity in cocaine dependence is not solely due to concomitant antisocial personality disorder and aggression, because increased impulsivity in cocaine-dependent subjects was observed with and without ASPD and aggression.

Impulsive behaviour is associated with low level of cerebrospinal fluid (CSF) 5- hydroxyindoleacetic acid (HIAA). Low CSF 5-HIAA has been shown to be present in DSH, so DSH may be biologically relevant in terms of impulsivity (Roy et al., 1989). Accordingly, Corruble et al. (1999) reported that DSH in depressed patients was associated with higher impulsivity than such behaviour in non-depressed patients.

Kreitman and Foster (1991) describe the commonest characteristics of DSH individuals as follows: strong dislike/invalidate themselves, hypersensitive to rejection, chronically angry usually at themselves, tend to suppress their anger, have high level of aggressive feelings, more impulsive and more lacking in impulse control, tend to act in accordance with their mood of the moment, tend not to plan for the future, tend towards irritability, do not see themselves as skilled at coping, do not have a flexible repertoire of coping skills, do not think they have much control over how/where they cope with life, and do not see themselves as empowered.

3.5 Deliberate Self-Harm and Suicide

Deliberate self-harm is distinct from suicide; the basic understanding is that a person who truly attempts suicide seeks to end all feelings, whereas a person who self-harms seeks to feel better; DSH is not a form of suicide but rather is a lifesaver (Herpertz, 1995). And because DSH and suicidal acts may blur; the DSH behaviours should be distinguished from those that are suicidal in nature. In DSH, the motivation is not intention to die, therefore, the debate is surrounding the person' intent to die or not (Herpertz, 1995). Suicide is not reported to provide relief as does DSH, and it is repeated less frequently than DSH. Although DSH behaviour is not suicidal in intent, it can lead to suicidal ideation. DSH has a strong association with suicide; in the year after an episode of DSH, the suicide rate is 100 times that of general population (Foster et al., 1997). Completed suicide in DSH is characterised by major depressive disorder, alcohol/drug abuse, and a past history of suicidal acts (Anderson, 1999).

There is much overlap of risk factors for DSH and suicide; there is also some dissimilarity. Suicide completers are more likely to be male, plan their attempts, use more dangerous methods, and suffer from persistent mental disorders such as depression (Harrington, 2001). Wilkinson and Smeeton (1987) stated that being male, older age, unemployed, living alone, poor physical health, psychiatric history, and previous attempts are all features that predict suicide. Suicide risk among DSH clients is hundreds of times higher than in the general population (Owens et al., 2002).

3.6 Deliberate Self-Harm and Crime

The rate of DSH among prisoners is much higher than among the general population (Liebling, 1993). Prison sitting may influence the methods of DSH chosen. Ireland (2000) reported that the majority of males offenders with DSH did so by cutting, hanging, and strangulation. Many studies reported that the rate of DSH is higher during the early periods of custody (Loucks, 1998). DSH was found in offenders with borderline personality disorders, substance abuse, and high level of impulsivity (Dolan, 2001).

The prisoners deliberately injure themselves because they cannot cope with life in jail. Some prisons recorded hundreds of incidents (Dolan, 2001).

Many studies have noted a desire among prison staff to distinguish between DSH and manipulative acts of self-harm, in which the goal is to gain attention or force a change in one's circumstances (Fleming et al., 1992). The desire to differentiate these two groups is based on the belief that each requires a different management response. DSH offenders require assistance and support, whereas manipulators should not have their behaviour reinforced; they should not obtain attention or a change in their circumstances (Fleming et al., 1992).

Dear et al. (2000) sought to determine whether DSH incidents classified as manipulative or attention-seeking would also be classified as low suicide intent and no risk to life. They found that prison staff cannot assume that prisoners who appear manipulative or who report manipulative motives were not suicidal at the time of self-harming. Which means manipulators in prison sitting may have some risk to life.

3.7 Repetition of Deliberate Self-Harm

As bizarre as it sounds, DSH has been reported to be an addiction (Shaw, 2002). Faye (1995) presented the development of a theory suggesting that DSH belongs in the realm of addictive behaviour. DSH exhibits numerous characteristics that have also been identified in the self-destructive behaviour of addiction. In line with other studies, Favazza and Conterio (1988) consider the role of neurotransmitters in addictive behaviour and the role of varying levels of neurotransmitters in diagnosis given to those individuals who harm themselves. Pembroke (2000) offers a challenge to this from the service-users perspective as one of 'psychological reductionism' when referring to the endorphin hypothesis of self-injury and alleged addiction to endogenous opioids. A further challenge to the 'addiction hypothesis' built on information previously discussed relates to the use of DSH as a coping mechanism. Faye (1995) describes DSH as 'crude, ultimately destructive coping mechanism, it is a mechanism that has many bad sides, but it works', and this could explain the attribution of addictive qualities. More acceptable coping mechanisms are repeated by individuals in circumstances of stress of personal difficulty without the self-destructive component. Faye (1995) suggested that less-destructive coping mechanisms are taught as a replacement and that these take time to become as effective as DSH. The repetition of DSH is common (Hawton et al., 1999). The risk factors for repetition of DSH are a history of DSH prior to the current episode, psychiatric history, current unemployment, low social class, alcohol- or drug-related problems, criminal record, antisocial personality, hopelessness, and suicidal intent (Wilkinson & Smeeton, 1987).

It is not surprising that DSH has been described as an addiction, because people are addicted to many things, from drugs to the Internet. Endorphins theory is one attempt in trying to decipher the mystery of the DSH . Habitually, the abused individual will self-mutilate because the flow of endorphins mimes that sensation one feels when they are loved (Pembroke, 2000). This, in turn, causes one to confuse abuse with love, self-abuse with self-love, because it is very difficult for the abused one to distinguish between love and abuse till it is very late. It is a tough habit to break, but it's a habit that must be broken.

3.8 Management of Deliberate Self-Harm

DSH behaviour is a complex issue. The evidence in terms of effective methods of management is inconclusive (Hawton, 1998). However, the management of individuals who engage in this behaviour should focus on three principle points. First is the immediate medical management of self-harming behaviour, involving appropriate medical care for those who have taken an overdose and dealing with medical complications associated with self-destructive behaviours. For example overdosing with paracetamol and the risk of liver failure is a particular problem in the UK as illustrated by Hawton et al. (1997); in order to solve the problem, paracetamol became available only in blister packs containing sixteen tablets. Packs of thirty-two tablets are available only in pharmacies (Hawton, 2002). Some data reported a reduction in the number of paracetamol overdosing subsequently and a decreased need for N-acetylcysteine and admissions to liver units (Boyce et al., 2001). Second, the aim should focus on preventing the recurrence of self-destructive behaviour, because there is a high risk of repetition of deliberate self-harm during the weeks immediately after an episode. Third, the underlying psychopathology needs assessment and treatment. Beautrais et al. (1996) noticed that during a month immediately before an attempt of DSH, 77% were depressed, 39% were abusing substances, 31% had contact or antisocial personality disorder, and 24% suffered from anxiety disorder.

Variety of pharmacological agents including selective sertonin reuptake inhibitors (SRRIs), mood stabilisers, and neuroleptics has been used (Illisse, 2002). Since antidepressant treatment alone is insufficient in preventing DSH (Haw et al., 2002), Heard (2000) suggested other treatments, including psychological interventions such as problem solving because most of DSH patients have poor problem-solving skills due to poor self-esteem and feelings of hopelessness. But Linehan et al. (2000) advise a more complex therapy for those with co-morbidity like dialectical behaviour therapy. For any treatment to be effective, it needs to be brief and focused, and the dialectical behaviour therapy is impractical for the majority of individuals with DSH behaviour, because it is an intensive intervention; therefore, two brief interventions have been introduced to people engaging in DSH: Manual Assisted Cognitive Therapy (MACT) and brief version of Cognitive Analytic Therapy (CAT). MACT is a brief, cognitively oriented, and problem-focused therapy. This therapy has been adapted from other such as dialectical behaviour therapy; it is effective in delaying the time of the next self-harming episode (Evans et al., 1999). CAT combines both cognitive and psychodynamic approaches; it is helpful as a tool for formulating the patient's self-harming behaviour and for clarifying and dealing with the counter-transference reactions, especially with borderline personality disorder (Sheard et al., 2000). Evans et al. (1999) and Sheard et al. (2000) stated that although both MACT and CAT are practical, a full evaluation is needed before it can be used in routine treatment of DSH.

The Emergency Department of the hospital is the first point of contact for the DSH people; therefore, effective training programmes should always be developed for accident and emergency staff dealing with DSH cases (Appleby et al., 2000). Direct discharge from A&E should only be contemplated if a psychological assessment and aftercare plan can be arranged in A&E prior to discharge. Specialist aftercare involves referral to psychiatric outpatient and social services (Hall, 1994; Yeo, 1993). Furthermore, the Royal College of Psychiatrists, in 1994, documented, the aim of clinical services for DSH as follows: to provide assessment and effective treatment of patient's physical condition; to provide a psychosocial assessment in order to identify those who have a psychiatric illness, a high suicide risk, those with co-morbid condition, and those in social crisis; to ensure prompt and effective psychiatric treatment and aftercare; and to insure the provision of social and psychological help for other psychosocial problems.

At present, it is not clear which interventions are helpful in reducing the repetition rates of DSH in depressed patients (Hawton et al., 1998).

3.9 Aims of the Study

The first aim of the study was to obtain information on socio-demographic characteristics of clients attending the Croydon & Lambeth, Southwark and Lewisham (LSL) Drug Treatment & Testing Orders Services (DTTO) that have a history of deliberate self-harm (DSH). The subsidiary aim was to investigate the relationship between DSH and substance misuse.

A few differences were hypothesised with respect to type, route of substance use, and DSH. Finally, the study explored the co-morbidity of DSH with depression/impulsivity, with the hypothesis that impulsivity was more likely to be observed in the DSH group.

4. Research Plan

4.1 Design

This small cross-sectional study was carried out in June and July 2003, at the Croydon & LSL DTTO Services. This survey obtained information on socio-demographic characteristics of clients who had a history of DSH and were attending the Croydon & LSL DTTO. It also investigated the relationship between the DSH and substance misuse. In addition, the study explored the co-morbidity of DSH with depression /impulsivity.

In a cross-sectional design, a sample is drawn from a population at a particular point in time. Information collected is used to describe the population at that time. This design can be used to assess interrelationships among variables within a population. This design is ideally suited to the descriptive and predictive functions associated with correlational research (Shaughnessy & Zechmeister, 1997). This type of the study is quick and relatively cheap to perform.

4.2 Setting

The study was carried out in an outpatient Croydon & LSL DTTO service, which is run by Croydon & LSL Probation service and the Maudsley Hospital Addictions Directorate.

The Drug Treatment and Testing Orders (DTTO) that was chosen as the research setting is a new community sentence, aimed at breaking the link between drug use and crime. It is a structured order for people who have a history of offending related to their substance misuse. The DTTO scheme was created by the United Kingdom Crime and Disorder Act 1998 and was piloted in three areas: Croydon, Liverpool, and Gloucestershire, until April 2000. After successful pilots, it was introduced nationally to every area in England. Information on all three DTTO pilot programmes is detailed in the Home Office final evaluation report (Turnbull et al., 2000). Under this recent governmental policy, substance-abusing offenders can be allowed to receive treatment as an alternative to custodial sentence. The effectiveness of that treatment can be monitored through mandatory urine or oral fluid screening, as well as through self-report and behavioural observation. Moreover, clients are assigned a key worker that monitors their progress and takes regular saliva fluid and provides social and psychological support.

4.3 Subjects

For the purpose of this study, a total of sixty male and female subjects attending the Croydon & LSL DTTO Services were sampled. The size of sample was decided based on a power calculation (using test of significance 0.05, standard deviation of 1.3 and power of 80%) after discussion with Ms Rebecca Welwyn, Bio-statistics IOP (Institute of Psychiatry), and was based upon the Nomogram (Gore & Altman, 1982).

Participants were consecutively recruited from attending the following DTTO service: Croydon & LSL. The clients attended the DTTO for one of the following reasons: for testing, to take prescriptions either methadone or buprenorphine, to be reviewed by a doctor, or to attend the psychological group (cognitive behavioural therapy, motivational interviewing, health education, stress management, relapse prevention, etc.). There was no age limit for subjects, but two exclusion criteria were applied in selecting the sample, namely clients who were psychotic and clients who were severely medically ill. Any client who at the time of the recruitment was sedated and/or was dysfunctional in any way was excluded at the time and was approached again on his next appointment in order to avoid biases and to prevent frustration. Finally, participation to the study was entirely voluntary. And the participators were offered £5 phone card as reimbursement for their time.

4.4 Research Instruments

A self-report semi-structured questionnaire comprising three parts was developed for the study. The first part included demographic characteristics of the subjects. The second part obtained data on substance misuse, and the third part dealt with the history of DSH in the sample (Appendix II). In addition, the clients filled out two standardised questionnaires, the *Beck Depression Inventory Scale* (BDI) (Beck et al., 1961) and the *Barratt Impulsiveness Scale* (BIS-11) (Patton et al., 1995).

The Beck Depression Inventory (BDI) is a self-administered twenty-one item self-report scale. Each item has a series of four statements, describing symptoms of depression along an ordinal continuum from absent or mild to severe. A total twenty-one symptoms are included (sadness, hopelessness, past failure, anhedonia, guilt, punishment, self-dislike, self-blame, suicidal thoughts, crying, irritability, loss of interest in activities, indecisiveness, self-image change, retardation in work, insomnia, fatigability, decreased appetite, loss of weight, somatic preoccupation, lack of interest in sex). Respondents are requested to rate the intensity of these symptoms on a scale from 0 to 3. Depression severity scores are created by summing the scores of the items endorsed from each item set. And the score levels are as follows: score <15 indicates mild depression, 15–30 indicates moderate depression, and score >30 indicates severe depression. The questionnaire takes approximately five to ten minutes to complete (Appendix III).

The Barratt Impulsiveness Scale (BIS-11) is a thirty-item self-report questionnaire divided into three subscales: attentional (inattention and cognitive instability), motor (motor impulsiveness and lack of perseverance), and non-planning (lack of self-control and intolerance of cognitive complexity (Barratt & Patton, 1983), and it has been designed to measure impulsiveness on a 4-point scale (1=Rarely/Never, 2=Occasionally, 3=Often, 4=Almost Always/Always). A score of 4 generally indicates the most impulsive response, but some items are scored in reverse order to avoid a response bias. The items are summed, and the higher the BIS-11 total score, the higher the impulsiveness level. The instrument takes ten minutes to complete (Appendix IV). An analysis of the scores was as follows. After taking the mean of the total scores which was seventy, scores were categorized in to three groups: low impulsivity from fifty-five to sixty-five, moderate impulsivity from sixty-six to seventy-one, and high impulsivity from seventy-two to ninety-one, and those categories were pre-approved by the author. The author was contacted by email, and he said that in the research and clinical studies, a score of seventy-five or higher is considered the cut-off point for high levels of impulsivity (Barratt, 2003). This shows that the categories done were appropriate for this sample study.

4.5 Procedures

The ethical approval of the study (by the appropriate NHS Trust Committee for purpose of an MSc in Clinical & Public Health Aspect of Addiction) was got by submitting the ethical approval form to Ethics Committee (Research) in February 2003 for review and approval prior to study commencement (Appendix VI).

After the permission from the ethical committee was granted, clients attending the Croydon & LSL DTTO Services were invited to participate in this research project by filling out the attached self-report questionnaires (Appendix II). Participants with a history of DSH completed the third part of the self-reported semi-structured questionnaire, which dealt with deliberate self-harm (DSH). Those without a history of DSH did not have to complete this part of the questionnaire.

Before visiting the outpatient DTTO service, the investigator contacted the consultant of the Croydon &LSL DTTO services and the DTTO manager either by telephone or by email. The aim of the study and any procedures were discussed and permission for carrying out the study in these places was requested. The ethical approval of the study was shown to them. Before recruiting any subjects, the researcher made sure, asking the people responsible, that no groups or one-to-one sessions were taking place at that time. This was done in order to ensure that treatment processes were not interrupted in any way. Before handing the subjects any questionnaires, they were first given a sheet containing relevant information about the study and information on their rights, as well as a consent sheet. In particular, they were told that their participation in the study was voluntary. Every opportunity was taken to explain to the clients what the study entailed and how the information they would provide would be kept in confidence. They were also given the chance to ask any questions and a full explanation was provided to allay any misgiving they had about taking part. Furthermore, they were assured that they had every right not to take part in the study, if they so wished. Not taking part would in no way affect their current treatment. It was explained that they had the right to withdraw from the study at any time without having to give any explanations. This information was clear in the information sheet and consent form (Appendix I).

Subjects were told that the result of the study could be given to them at the end of the study if they requested this. If they agreed to participate in the study, they were asked to sign the consent form. After that, all subjects, each on an individual basis, were given the questionnaires. The subjects were asked to fill these in themselves. Two subjects were illiterate, so the questions were read out to them and filled in by the researcher. The investigator was present during the whole procedure to answer any possible questions and provide further details if necessary. The questionnaires were clear and easy to understand except part two of the semi-structure questionnaire, which dealt with substance use. Twelve clients had difficulty in understanding this, especially the section that asked about frequency of using substance. Since the beginning of the study and until the recruitment of the sample was finished, seven clients refused to participate. One withdrew before completing the questionnaire, and two clients took the questionnaire and promised to bring it by next appointment but, unfortunately, did not show up. Among the seven who initially refused to take part, three came for their next appointments and spontaneously asked to fill out the questionnaire, which they did.

It was thought that completion of the questionnaires would take approximately thirty minutes for every subject. However, the majority of the clients completed the questionnaire in fifteen to twenty minutes if they had history of DSH. Clients with no history of DSH it took ten to fifteen to fill the questionnaire.

After filling the questionnaire, each subject was given a £5 phone card and was asked to sign a sheet to confirm they had received the phone card (Appendix V).

A total of sixty clients took part, twenty-two from the Croydon DTTO and thirty-eight from the LSL DTTO. The difference in the size of sample in each DTTO depended on the number of clients registered in each one. The LSL DTTO had more registered clients so it was busier.

4.6 Statistical Analysis

Standard statistical tests – chi-square and logistic regression tests – were used to analyse the obtained data to assess difference in proportions. These methods are considered the best measures to evaluate statistically the relationships between different variables even in small samples. Values of $P < 0.05$ were considered as statistically significant.

All statistical tests were based on the STATA statistical software package (Windows, version 6), which has complete statistical, graphical, and data-management capabilities.

5. Results

5.1 Demographic Characteristics

A total of sixty subjects were recruited in this study, sixty subjects, fifty-three males and seven females (M: F = 7.6:1). Their ages ranged from 20–50 years, and the mean age was 33.9 years (standard deviation of 7.2). The study population was predominantly white male, single (n= 40, 66.7%), with no qualifications (n=37, 61.7%) and unemployed (n=57, 95%). Moreover, seventeen (28.3%) lived in Council estates, twelve (20%) in rented flats, eleven (18.3%) in hostels, eight (13.3%) had their own houses, and twelve (20%) were called 'other' category which included supported housing (1), housing trust (1), staying with friends (1), staying with mother (1), and no fixed abode (8).

Of the sixty clients, thirty-nine had a history of DSH; thirty-four were males and five were females (M: F= 7:1). Their ages ranged from twenty-one to fifty years (Mean age =34.5 years ± SD = 7.1 years). Due to the wide range of ages, they were divided into two groups, under and above the age of thirty-five years. Questions an ethnic background revealed that the sample was mainly white clients (n=24, 61.5%) followed by black (n=9, 23.1%). Clients from Middle East (n=4, 10.3%) and mixed ethnic ancestry (black and white) (n=2, 5.1%) were grouped together and called 'Others'. The highest qualification was the University degree. And the mean age of leaving school with a history of DSH and non-DSH was 15.2 years.

Demographic information (including gender, age, ethnicity, marital status, qualification, education level, employment status, year since last employed, and home status) of subjects with DSH and non-DSH is summarised in (Appendix VII, Table 1).

5.2 DTTO Offenders

The majority of the clients were funding their substance use by shoplifting, and they were ordered for DTTO due to shoplifting (n=33, 55%); other reasons for DTTO were thirteen burglary, three theft, two deception, one fraud. One failed to appear at DTTO service, and seven were not specified. And 58/60 (96.7%) of the sample reported a history of imprisonment in the past. Out of the thirty three (55%) shoplifters, twenty-one (63.6%) offenders were with a history DSH (Table 1).

Table 1: Reason, length of current DTTO, and length of previous time in prison of Croydon and LSL DTTO offenders.

DTTO offenders	DSH (n=39, 100%)	Non-DSH (n=21, 100%)	Total (n=60, 100%)
Reason for DTTO			
Shoplifting	21 (53.9)	12 (57.1)	33 (55.0)
Burglary	8 (20.5)	5 (23.8)	13 (21.7)
Other	10 (25.6)	4 (19.1)	14 (23.3)
Length of current DTTO (in years)			
1	19 (48.7)	12 (57.1)	31 (51.7)
1.5	19 (48.7)	8 (38.1)	27 (45.0)
2	1 (2.6)	1 (4.8)	2 (3.3)
Length of previous prison (in years)			
< 1	15 (38.5)	14 (66.7)	29 (48.3)
1–6	13 (33.3)	3 (14.3)	16 (26.7)
> 6	9 (23.1)	4 (19.0)	13 (21.7)
None	2 (5.1)	0 (0.0)	2 (3.3)

DSH: Deliberate Self-Harm.

DTTO: Drug Treatment and Testing Order.

5.3 Substance Use

The majority of clients reported a history of alcohol consumption. Both groups reported a history of early age of consumption as early as seven years old. There were eight clients in each group who did not report a history of drinking alcohol, which is an unexpected finding (Table 2).

Table 2: Detailed data about consumption of alcohol in both groups.

Substance used (Alcohol)	DSH (n=39, 100%)	Non-DSH (n=21, 100%)	Total (%) (n=60, 100%)
Ever used alcohol			
Yes	31 (79.5)	13 (61.9)	44 (73.3)
No	8 (20.5)	8 (38.1)	16 (26.7)
Age at first use (in years)			
Not using	8 (20.5)	8 (38.1)	16 (26.7)
7–12	12 (30.8)	5 (23.8)	17 (28.3)
13–18	19 (48.7)	8 (38.1)	27 (45.0)
Last time used			
Not using	8 (20.5)	8 (38.1)	16 (26.7)
One day ago	12 (30.8)	6 (28.6)	18 (30.0)
Seven days ago	8 (20.5)	1 (4.8)	9 (15.0)
More than seven days ago	5 (12.8)	0 (0.0)	5 (8.3)
No answer	6 (15.4)	6 (28.6)	12 (20.0)
Frequency of use			
Not using	8 (20.5)	8 (38.1)	16 (26.7)
Daily	13 (33.3)	5 (23.8)	18 (30.0)
Social	7 (18.0)	1 (4.8)	8 (13.3)
No answer	11 (28.2)	7 (33.3)	18 (30.0)
Typical amount daily use (in pounds)			
Not using	8 (20.5)	8 (38.1)	16 (26.7)
<6	14 (35.9)	5 (23.8)	19 (31.7)
6–10	5 (12.8)	1 (4.8)	6 (10.0)
>10	2 (5.1)	0 (0.0)	2 (3.3)
No answer	10 (25.7)	7 (33.3)	17 (28.3)

DSH: Deliberate Self-Harm.

The majority of the clients in both groups were using heroin (n=34, 87.2%, and n=16, 76.2%, respectively) on a daily basis. Out of both groups, 27 (45%) clients gave a history of using heroin one day prior to filling the questionnaire. Thirty (50%) clients were smoking/chasing heroin, and 20 (33.3%) were injecting it (Table 3).

Table 3: Detailed data about use of heroin in both groups.

Substance used (Heroin)	DSH (n=39, 100%)	Non-DSH (%) (n=21, 100%)	Total (n=60, 100%)
Ever used heroin			
Yes	34 (87.2)	16 (76.2)	50 (83.3)
No	5 (12.8)	5 (23.8)	10 (16.7)
Age at first use (in years)			
Not using	5 (12.8)	5 (23.8)	10 (16.7)
13–19	15 (38.5)	10 (47.6)	25 (41.7)
20–40	19 (48.7)	6 (28.6)	25 (41.7)
Last time used			
Not using	5 (12.8)	5 (23.8)	10 (16.7)
One day ago	17 (43.6)	10 (47.6)	27 (45.0)
Seven days ago	3 (7.7)	1 (4.8)	4 (6.7)
More than seven days ago	9 (23.1)	4 (19.0)	13 (21.7)
No answer	5 (12.8)	1 (4.8)	6 (10.0)
Frequency of use			
Not using	5 (12.8)	5 (23.8)	10 (16.7)
Daily	24 (61.5)	10 (47.6)	34 (56.7)
Weekly	2 (5.1)	2 (9.5)	4 (6.7)
No answer	8 (20.5)	4 (19.0)	12 (20.0)
Typical amount in daily use (in pounds)			
Not using	5 (12.8)	5 (23.8)	10 (16.7)
<40	11 (28.2)	12 (57.1)	23 (38.3)
40–100	11 (28.2)	2 (9.5)	13 (21.7)
>100	5 (12.8)	1 (4.8)	6 (10.0)
No answer	7 (18.0)	1 (4.8)	8 (13.3)
Route of administration			
Not using	5 (12.8)	5 (23.8)	10 (16.7)
Smoke/Chase	19 (48.7)	11 (52.4)	30 (50.0)
Inject	15 (38.5)	5 (23.8)	20 (33.3)
No answer	0 (0.00)	0 (0.0)	0 (0.0)

DSH: Deliberate Self-Harm.

Most of the clients in both groups were using cocaine powder or crack cocaine (smoking/snorting). However, 13/60 (21.7%) were injecting it. Twenty (33.3%) clients were spending more than £100 in typical day use (Table 4).

Table 4: Detailed data about use of cocaine/crack in both groups.

Substance used (Cocaine/Crack)	DSH (n=39, 100%)	Non-DSH (n=21, 100%)	Total (n=60, 100%)
Ever used cocaine/crack			
Yes	36 (92.3)	20 (95.2)	56 (93.3)
No	3 (7.7)	1 (4.8)	4 (6.7)
Age at first use (in years)			
Not using	3 (7.7)	1 (4.8)	4 (6.7)
13–19	15 (38.5)	6 (28.6)	21 (35.0)
20–40	21 (53.8)	14 (66.7)	35 (58.3)
Last time used			
Not using	3 (7.7)	1 (4.8)	4 (6.7)
One day ago	13 (33.3)	10 (47.6)	23 (38.3)
Seven days ago	8 (20.5)	4 (19.0)	12 (20.0)
More than seven days ago	12 (30.8)	2 (9.5)	14 (23.3)
No answer	3 (7.7)	4 (19.1)	7 (11.7)
Frequency of use			
Not using	3 (7.7)	1 (4.8)	4 (6.7)
Daily	22 (56.4)	8 (38.1)	30 (50.0)
Weekly	5 (12.8)	5 (23.8)	10 (16.7)
No answer	9 (23.1)	7 (33.3)	16 (26.7)
Typical amount in daily use (in pounds)			
Not using	3 (7.7)	1 (4.8)	4 (6.7)
<40	9 (23.1)	10 (47.6)	19 (31.7)
40–100	7 (18.0)	2 (9.5)	9 (15.0)
>100	14 (35.9)	6 (28.6)	20 (33.3)
No answer	6 (15.4)	2 (9.5)	8 (13.3)
Route of administration			
Not using	3 (7.7)	1 (4.8)	4 (6.7)
Smoke/Snort	27 (69.2)	15 (71.4)	42 (70.0)
Inject	9 (23.1)	4 (19.0)	13 (21.7)
No answer	0 (0.00)	1 (4.8)	1 (1.7)

DSH: Deliberate Self-Harm.

From the total of forty-nine (81.7%) who were using cannabis, only seven (11.7%) clients were spending more than £20 daily on cannabis (Table 5).

Table 5: Detailed data about use of cannabis in both groups.

Substance used(Cannabis)	DSH (n=39, 100%)	Non-DSH (n=21, 100%)	Total (n=60, 100%)
Ever used cannabis			
Yes	33 (84.6)	16 (76.2)	49 (81.7)
No	6 (15.4)	5 (23.8)	11 (18.3)
Age at first use (in years)			
Not using	6 (15.4)	5 (23.8)	11 (18.3)
10–14	21 (53.8)	9 (42.9)	30 (50.0)
15–30	12 (30.8)	7 (33.3)	19 (31.7)
Last time used			
Not using	6 (15.4)	5 (23.8)	11 (18.3)
One day ago	15 (38.5)	7 (33.3)	22 (36.7)
Seven days ago	7 (17.9)	3 (14.3)	10 (16.7)
More than seven days ago	7 (17.9)	0 (0.0)	7 (11.7)
No answer	4 (10.3)	6 (28.6)	10 (16.7)
Frequency of use			
Not using	6 (15.4)	5 (23.8)	11 (18.3)
Daily	19 (48.7)	6 (28.6)	25 (41.7)
Weekly	9 (23.1)	6 (28.6)	15 (25.0)
No answer	5 (12.8)	4 (19.0)	9 (15.0)
Typical amount in daily use (in pounds)			
Not using	6 (15.4)	5 (23.8)	11 (18.3)
<10	14 (35.9)	8 (38.1)	22 (36.7)
10–20	7 (18.0)	0 (0.0)	7 (11.7)
>20	5 (12.8)	2 (9.5)	7 (11.7)
No answer	7 (17.9)	6 (28.6)	13 (21.7)

DSH: Deliberate Self-Harm.

Only 24/60 (40%) clients were using benzodiazepines, and 6/24 (25%) users were using more than 40 mg on a daily basis (Table 6).

Table 6: Detailed data about use of benzodiazepines in both groups.

Substance used (benzodiazepines)	DSH (n=39, 100%)	Non-DSH (n=21, 100%)	Total (n=60, 100%)
Ever used benzodiazepines			
Yes	17 (43.6)	7 (33.3)	24 (40.0)
No	22 (56.4)	14 (66.7)	36 (60.0)
Age at first use (in years)			
Not using	22 (56.4)	14 (66.7)	36 (60.0)
13–19	9 (23.1)	4 (19.0)	13 (21.7)
20–34	8 (20.5)	3 (14.3)	11 (18.3)
Last time used			
Not using			
One day ago	22 (56.4)	14 (66.7)	36 (60.0)
Seven days ago	4 (10.3)	3 (14.3)	7 (11.7)
More than seven days ago	4 (10.3)	2 (9.5)	6 (10.0)
No answer	5 (12.8)	0 (0.0)	5 (8.3)
	4 (10.3)	2 (9.5)	6 (10.0)
Frequency of use			
Not using	22 (56.4)	14 (66.7)	36 (60.0)
Daily	7 (18.0)	2 (9.5)	9 (15.0)
Weekly	3 (7.7)	1 (4.8)	4 (6.7)
No answer	7 (17.9)	4 (19.0)	11 (18.3)
Typical amount in daily use (in mg)			
Not using	22 (56.4)	14 (66.7)	36 (60.0)
< 40	4 (10.3)	4 (19.0)	8 (13.3)
>40	5 (12.8)	1 (4.8)	6 (10.0)
No answer	8 (20.5)	2 (9.5)	10 (16.7)

DSH: Deliberate Self-Harm.

Other substances included lysergic acid diethylamide (LSD)/Ecstasy (6), amphetamines (3), barbiturate (1), and opium (1) (Table 7).

Table 7: Detailed data about use of other substances in both groups.

Substance used (other)	DSH (n=39, 100%)	Non-DSH (n=21, 100%)	Total (n=60, 100%)
Ever used other substance			
Yes	9 (23.1)	7 (33.3)	11 (18.3)
No	30 (76.9)	14 (66.7)	49 (81.7)
Age at first use (in years)			
Not using	30 (76.9)	19 (90.5)	49 (81.7)
11–19	6 (15.4)	2 (9.5)	8 (13.3)
20–23	3 (7.7)	0 (0.0)	3 (5.0)
Last time used			
Not using	30 (76.9)	19 (90.5)	49 (81.7)
One day ago	2 (5.1)	0 (0.0)	2 (3.3)
Seven days ago	1 (2.6)	0 (0.0)	1 (1.7)
More than seven days ago	1 (2.6)	1 (4.8)	2 (3.3)
No answer	5 (12.8)	1 (4.8)	6 (10.0)
Frequency of use			
Not using	30 (76.9)	19 (90.5)	49 (81.7)
Daily	2 (5.1)	0 (0.0)	2 (3.3)
Occasionally	2 (5.1)	0 (0.0)	2 (3.3)
No answer	5 (12.8)	2 (9.5)	7 (11.7)
Typical amount in daily use			
Not using	30 (76.9)	19 (90.5)	49 (81.7)
No answer	9 (23.1)	2 (9.5)	11(18.3)

DSH: Deliberate Self-Harm.

The preferred substance among the above was heroin for both groups.

Other substances included Amphetamine (2), Opium (1), and Benzodiazepines (1) (Table 8)

Table 8: Details of preferred substance use in both groups.

Preferred substance used	DSH (n=39, 100%)	Non-DSH (n=21, 100%)	Total (n=60, 100%)
Cannabis	1 (2.3)	5 (23.8)	6 (10.0)
Cocaine	3 (7.7)	0 (0.0)	3 (5.0)
Crack	9 (23.1)	5 (23.8)	14 (23.3)
Heroin	14 (35.9)	9 (42.9)	**23 (38.3)**
Crack/Heroin	8 (20.5)	2 (9.5)	10 (16.7)
Other	4 (5.1)	0 (0.0)	4 (6.7)

DSH: Deliberate Self-Harm.

5.4 Relationship between DSH and Non-DSH and Other Variables Measured

In order to take into account a variety of variables that might be associated with DSH, and to define their interaction, chi-square test statistical model was performed. Each demographic factor was collapsed in to two or three categories according to higher number of each one for the purpose of the analysis. Fisher's exact p-value was used, and the significant level was <0.05.

The result of the analysis in this study indicated that none of the demographic factors were found to be significant predictors for DSH (Appendix VII, Table 2).

It was also found that there was no association between DSH and the type of substance used, client's age at first use, and the route of the administration, when each substance was examined independently from each other (all gave p >0.05) (Appendix VII, Table 3)

In contrast, there was a significant association between DSH and preferred substance use, which showed heroin as positive most preferred substance (p = 0.025) (Table 9).

Table 9: Relationship between DSH and non-DSH and preferred substance use.

Preferred substance use	DSH (39)	Non-DSH (21)	Chi 2	P-value
Preferred substance use				
Cannabis	1	5		
Crack	9	5		
Heroin	14	9	**11.095**	**0.025**
Crack/Heroin	8	2		
Other	7	0		

Bold font indicates significant relationship.

df =4

In addition, DSH was further examined with all variables in the Appendix VII, Table 3 by using logistic regression, and it still did not show any significant associations (data not shown) except for preferred substance used that was heroin, Table 10.

Table 10: Relationship between DSH and non-DSH and a preferred substance use.

Preferred substance use	Odds Ratio	P-value	95% Confidence. Interval
Cannabis	1.00	-	-
Crack	17.765	0.078	0.721–437.886
Heroin	**30.543**	**0.043**	**1.122–831.391**
Crack/Heroin	6.757	0.261	0.242–188.574
Other	22.571	0.086	0.642–793.837

Bold font: Indicates significant relationship.

5.5 Co-morbidity of the DSH and Non-DSH with Impulsiveness and Depression

This study showed that there were no significant correlations between DSH and BIS-11 and BDI. However, DSH clients scored higher in the severe impulsive category than the non-DSH clients (Appendix VII, Table 4).

Furthermore, there was no significant association between severe impulsive category and severe depression category, as p-value was 0.605.

It should be added that the multivariable (Impulsive and Depression) were measured together by using logistic regression test and it did not show any significant association with DSH (Appendix VII, Table 5).

5.6 Deliberate Self-Harm (DSH)

Within the DSH-related questionnaires, it was found that the mean age at first episode of DSH was 23.2 years (standard deviation of 6.5), and 11/39 (28.2%) had harmed themselves from four to ten times in the past. Only 6/39 (15.4%) had an episode of DSH in the last month, and the majority (n=31, 79.5%) did not harm themselves in front of others(Table 11).

Table 11: History of DSH of the clients attending the Croydon and LSL DTTO service.

DSH	Male (n=34, 100%)	Female (n=5, 100%)	Total (n=39, 100%)
Age at first DSH			
10–21	15 (44.1)	4 (80.0)	19 (48.7)
22–39	19 (55.9)	1 (20.0)	20 (51.3)
Frequency of DSH in the past			
1–3 times			
4–10 times	25 (73.5)	3 (60.0)	28 (71.8)
	9 (26.5)	2 (40.0)	11 (28.2)
DSH in the last month			
Yes	5 (14.7)	1 (20.0)	6 (15.4)
No	29 (85.3)	4 (80.0)	33 (84.6)
DSH in front of others			
Yes	8 (23.5)	0 (0.00)	8 (20.5)
No	26 (76.5)	5 (100.0)	31 (79.5)

DSH: Deliberate Self-Harm.

The commonest methods of DSH were cutting and overdosing. Among the twenty-one (53.9%) who cut themselves; seventeen cut their wrist, two their abdomen, one the anterior left chest in the region of the heart, and one his arm. With respect to overdose, nine had overdosed with heroin, and eleven overdosed with other drugs (not specified). The 'other' category of DSH methods included one burning, one hanging, one inhaling car fumes, and one drinking fuel (Figure 1).

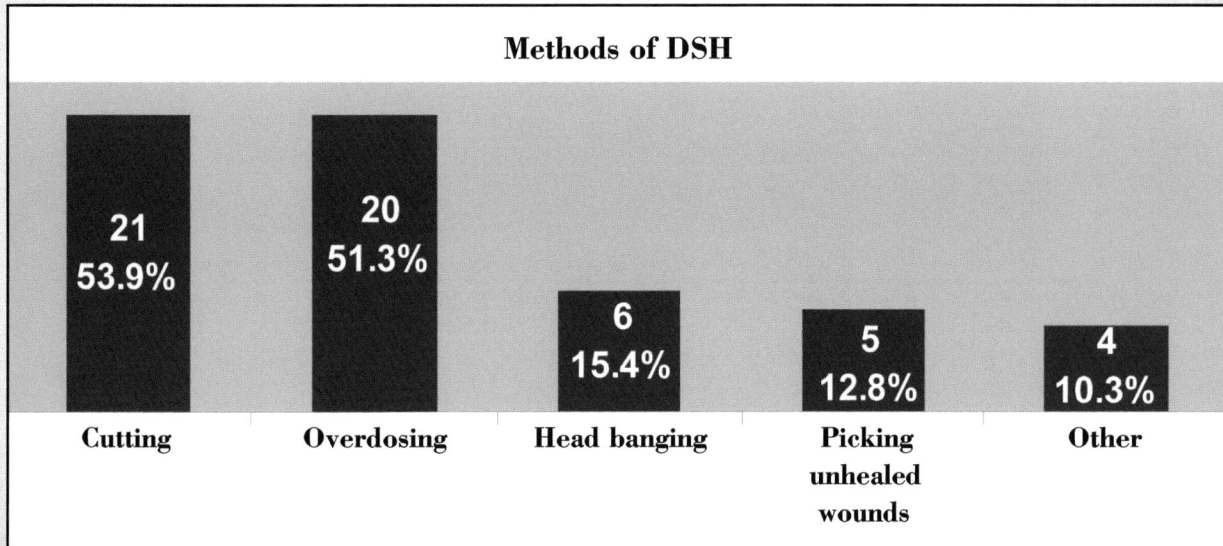

Figure 1: Different methods of DSH reported by clients attending the Croydon and LSL DTTO Services.

Emotional pain (n=25, 64.1%) was frequently experienced by the clients before the episode of DSH. The 'other' category included one depression and four not specified (Figure 2).

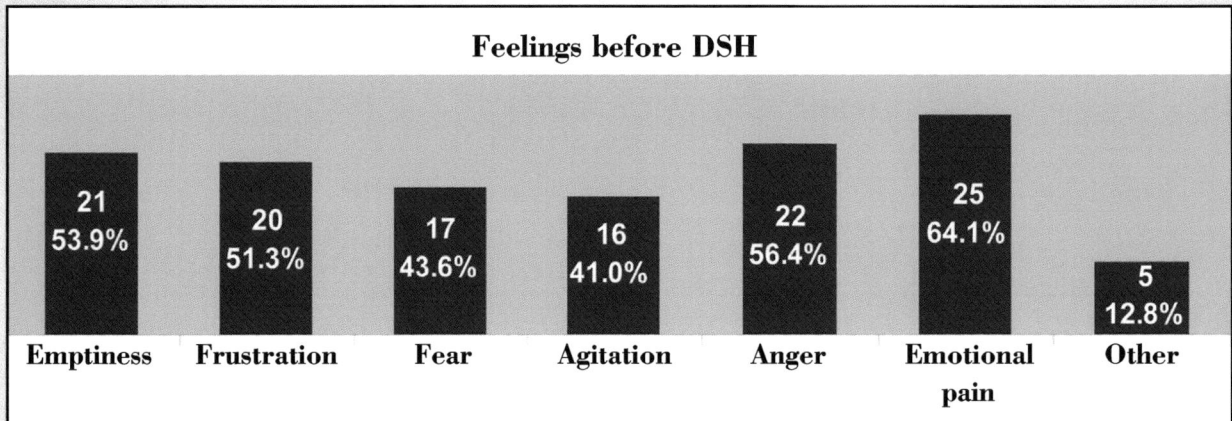

Feelings before DSH

Emptiness	Frustration	Fear	Agitation	Anger	Emotional pain	Other
21 53.9%	20 51.3%	17 43.6%	16 41.0%	22 56.4%	25 64.1%	5 12.8%

Figure 2: Different feelings experienced by clients before the episode of DSH.

Regretfulness (n=16, 41%) was the most frequent emotion experienced by the clients after the episode of DSH. The 'other' category included two stupid, one selfish, and one desperate (Figure 3).

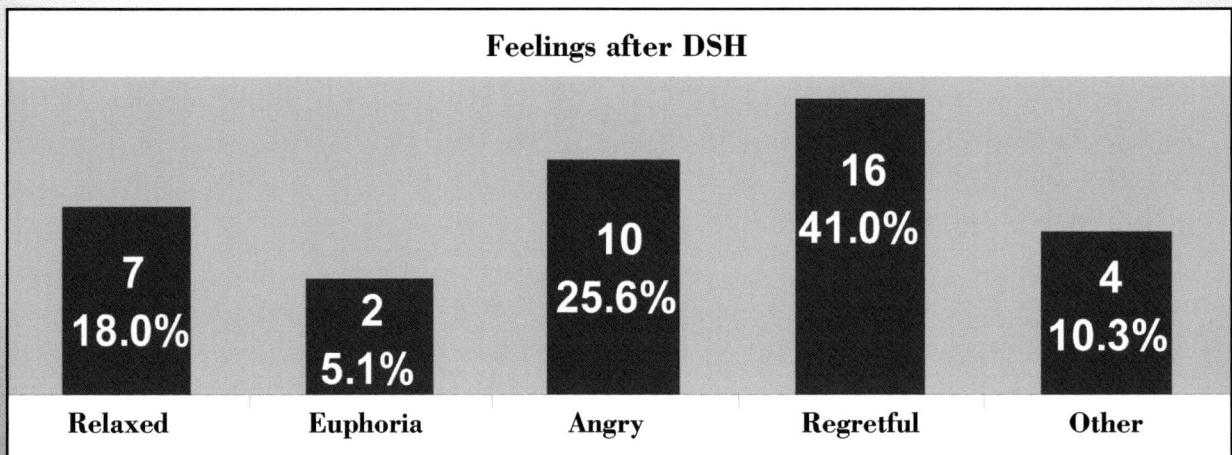

Feelings after DSH

Relaxed	Euphoria	Angry	Regretful	Other
7 18.0%	2 5.1%	10 25.6%	16 41.0%	4 10.3%

Figure 3: Different feelings experienced by the clients after an episode of DSH.

Drugs (n=26, 66.7%) were the most common factor precieved to have provoked the episode of DSH. The 'other' category included one family problem, one thinking of past (Figure 4).

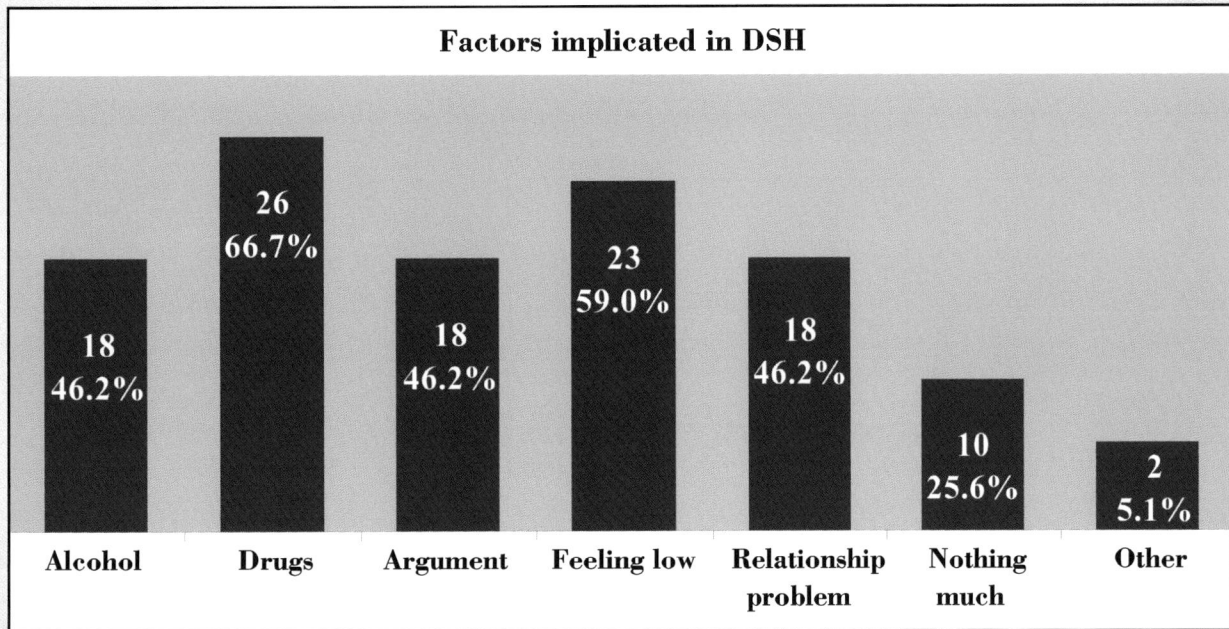

Factors implicated in DSH

Alcohol — 18, 46.2%
Drugs — 26, 66.7%
Argument — 18, 46.2%
Feeling low — 23, 59.0%
Relationship problem — 18, 46.2%
Nothing much — 10, 25.6%
Other — 2, 5.1%

Figure 4: Factors perceived to have provoked the episode of DSH.

The majority of the DSH act (n=15, 38.5%) were done without the clients feeling any physical pain. Only eight (20.5%) clients had severe pain. Most clients (n=26, 66.7%) revealed that more than 50% of their DSH was carried out under the influence of alcohol and drugs, and the vast majority (n=31, 79.5%) stated that the effect of alcohol and drugs make worse the episode of DSH (Appendix VII, Table 6).

Most of the clients (n=22, 56.4%) did not seek any medical treatment after the DSH. Twenty-five (64.1%) of the clients had never been referred to a psychiatrist, and twenty-nine (74.4%) had never been followed up by general psychiatrist or any member of a liaison psychiatry team. Among those who received treatment by medical staff in the Accident and Emergency (A&E) Department, twelve (30.8%) felt that they had been ignored, and eleven (28.2%) felt that the staff been angry with them (Appendix VII, Table 7).

Responders were asked if they wanted to stop self-harming. The vast majority (n=36, 92.3%) of clients reported that they needed to stop self-harming and gave different reasons; nine to live, three said that it is mad, two said it leads to scars and it does not look good, two said for the sake of children, one said that it is bad because it leads to infection, one called it stupid, and twenty-two did not specify.

The three clients, who did not want to stop, did not give any reason for this answer. The majority of clients reported that there were many things that prevented them from feeling the need to self-harm. Being drug-free and having family support were the main reasons given.

And when they were asked how to know when to stop self-harming, the following answers were given: fifteen did not know, five said when it hurts, two said by realizing what was done was mad, one said when the heart pumps fast, one when getting consciousness back, and fourteen did not specify.

Most of the DSH clients (n=26, 66.7%) also had experienced suicidal thoughts. Fifteen were not sure if suicide was associated with DSH. Nineteen had actually made true suicidal attempts. This included seven cases of overdosing, three of jumping from a bridge, one cutting deeply the wrist, and seven not specified (Appendix VII, Table 8).

Responders were also asked how many times they had suicidal thoughts and suicidal acts; the results are shown in Table 12.

Table 12: Suicidal thoughts and suicidal acts.

Suicidal thoughts (in times)	Number of clients
1–3	14
4–6	4
>6	2
Not specified	6
Suicidal acts (in times)	**Number of clients**
1–2	9
3–4	8
Not specified	2

Most DSH clients (n=32, 82.1%) had a traumatic past experience, including nine sexual, seven mental, and six physical abuse by others, and two the loss of parents, two family problems, one racism, one losing best friend, one being bullied at school, one, one of parents being alcoholic, and one being adapted at children house reported by few clients as a traumatic experience.

Of the thirty-nine clients, nineteen (23.1%) had been diagnosed with mental illness, fourteen with depression, three with eating disorder, and one other not specified (Appendix VII, Table 8).

Ever use of heroin in DSH group was further examined separately with some variables of the questionnaire that it was expected to be associated more than the others. To measure the association of different variables (using of alcohol, using of crack/cocaine, using of cannabis, using of benzodiazepines, using of other drugs, methods of DSH like cutting/overdosing, pain during DSH, feelings (emotional pain) before DSH, feelings (regretful) after DSH, medical staffs' attitude, suicidal ideation, past traumatic experience (sexual abuse), diagnosed mental illness (depression/ eating disorder), length of DTTO, and pervious time in prison) recorded in participated clients in relation of using heroin (as a main factor) in the DSH group, logistic regression was performed (Appendix VII, Table 9).

None showed it to be associated with using heroin in DSH group except alcohol use, which showed that heroin users who deliberately self-harm themselves are also nine times more likely to be alcohol users.

These variables were chosen by the investigator to be compared to heroin in self-reported DSH, because either it was expected that an association would be found between them, and it was of particular interest that their association be explored.

And to find out the relationship of heroin and alcohol users in the non-DSH group, logistic regression was performed again, and it did not show any significant association (Table 13).

Table 13: Relationship of heroin and alcohol users for DSH and non-DSH groups.

	Odds Ratio	P-value	95% Confidence Interval
Ever used Alcohol (DSH)			
Yes			
No	**8.7**	**0.036**	**1.148–65.932**
Ever used Alcohol (Non-DSH)			
Yes			
No	1.1	0.920	0.142–8.680

Bold font: indicates significant association.

6. Discussion

Of the sixty clients approached, thirty-nine had a history of DSH, and the other twenty-one clients didn't. A reason for this may be because the study predominately involved male population and most studies show a correlation between females and DSH. Some studies show that DSH especially 'cutting' was common in the male prison population. A DTTO sample is likely to include less DSH. Clients may have underestimated their DSH as this issue is a sensitive one, and they might also have wanted to save time when they knew that they would escape the part III of the questionnaire if they gave no history of DSH.

6.1 Substance Use and Deliberate Self-Harm

An unexpected finding of this study was that sixteen of the clients had no history of ever having used alcohol. It seems that they did not see their alcohol use as a problem, so they didn't answer that question. Another interesting finding was that none had put alcohol as a preferred substance; multiple substance users always preferred illicit drugs to alcohol.

The study showed that (n=27) 45% of heroin users and (n=23) 38.3% of cocaine/crack users gave a history of using the above substance one day prior of filling the questionnaire, although that was surprising. However, it is not to show the downside of the DTTO service and its aims and goals because abstinence from drugs does not necessarily a make a successful DTTO. A successful DTTO is to make positive lifestyle changes; stop offending; start looking after their self; re-establish relationships with family members or stay in a long-term relationship, which can lead to a permanent employment; better housing situation; moving gradually away from offending behaviour and developing more pro-social activities and returning to a normal lifestyle as a society would expect one to do or enter into.

The result of the study also showed that (n=30) 50% of heroin users were smoking/chasing it and less number of clients (n=20) 33.3% were injecting it, and a similar finding with cocaine/crack users showed that (n=42) 70% were smoking/snorting it and only (n=13) 21.7% were injecting it. This may indicate that the ones who adopted high-risk behaviour by injecting changed to a low-risk behaviour by smoking. Any reduction in drug use, change in route of administration of drugs, reduction in typical amount spent on drugs, or a change in the source of funding the drugs other than crime (through benefits or legitimate means) would all play a major role in crime reduction on a long-term basis and would be considered a success for DTTO service.

Current study revealed that more than 50% of DSH episodes occurred under the influence of alcohol and illicit drug use. This insures the strong link between the DSH and substance use as other studies have documented (Dhossche et al., 2000; Haw et al., 2001; Powis et al., 1999; Wily et al., 1996).

The main finding of this small-scale pilot study indicates that the preferred substance of abuse (heroin) was significantly associated with DSH. However, this study did not indicate any association in the type or the route of administration of the drugs with DSH, as other studies have previously shown. When the question about most-preferred drug was asked, heroin came on top. But when asked in detail about drug habit, no single drug was found in statistically significant manner. It just shows the unreliability of self-reporting. In this incidence, the leading question forced the client to make a preference, but his/her own detailed description drug use did not reveal statistically significant drug of choice.

6.2 Impulsivity and Deliberate Self-Harm

DSH clients scored higher in high level of impulsivity, which was in ascendance with other studies (Holdsworth et al., 2001; Zaidan et al., 2002) On the contrary, DSH clients scored higher in mild depression category, which means that the DSH acts are more impulsive than depressive, although the statistical analysis didn't show any significant association. It is important to remember that the relationship, which is not statistically significant, can be clinically significant and vice versa.

Impulsiveness is an inheritable personality trait associated with serotonin function (Schalling et al., 1984). A number of genetic polymorphisms have been identified that may alter serotonin function.

Nielsen et al. (1998) found a link between tryptopan hydroxylase (TPH) intron 7 polymorphism and impulsive DSH acts in a population of alcoholic and violent offenders. Serotonin inhibitors produced increased impulse/aggression behaviour; serotonin exciters decreased in aggression. The exact type of impulse/aggression behaviour shown in response to irritation depends on levels of serotonin. If they are normal, irritation might be expressed by screaming, throwing things. However, if the serotonin level is low, impulse/aggression increases and responses to irritation lead to DSH, suicide, or attack on others. Evans at al. (2000) reported the significant relationship between impulsiveness and TPH genotype in males. Biological/neurochemistry is one of the aetiologies of DSH. However, no one has all the pieces of the puzzle, and it's naive to think that DSH behaviour is solely environmentally controlled or only the result of biological mechanism. Any behaviour is determined by both environment and biological factors.

6.3 Methods of Deliberate Self-Harm

Results demonstrate that the commonest methods of DSH were cutting and overdosing. Among the twenty-one (53.9%) who cut themselves, seventeen cut their wrists. This shows that the most common site for cutting is the wrist as reported by Rosen and Heard (1995). The location of the wound on the body is a useful addition when describing a DSH act. There are obvious differences between a cut made to the wrist versus one made on the face or genitals. The location of the wound is relevant to both assessing lethality and designing treatment. It is also possible that individuals who inflict superficial injuries are of different populations than those who engage in more serious acts of DSH (Rosen & Heard, 1995). Studies by Holdsworth (2001) and Townsend et al. 2001 (studied all individuals presented to a general hospital for DSH between 1985 & 1997) and the current study, all show that overdose is still the commonest method of DSH. Methods less frequently reported included burning and interference with wound healing – in current study as well as in previous study (Favazza & Conterio, 1988).

Methods of DSH depend on many factors (Favazza & Conterio, 1988): availability, source of the sample (DTTO offenders differ from a prison population), type of the clients (mentally retarded individual, psychotic patients, individual with character disorder such as borderline personality disorder), etc.

6.4 The Emotional and Physical Pains with Deliberate Self-Harm

Emotional pain was the most frequent emotion experienced by the clients before the episode of DSH. Self-harmers believe that when intense feelings build up and when they are unable to cope, by self-injury and causing pain, they reduce the level of emotional and physical arousal to a bearable one. They distract from the internal pain by mirroring internal pain with external pain (Smith et al., 1998). They believe that dealing with physical pain is easier than dealing with emotional pain. DSH is a symbol of their emotional pain.

The experience of pain varies among those who harmed themselves. Absolute analgesia for the event was commonly described in this study (n=15, 38.5%). Similar finding was found by Winchel and Stanley (1991) and Favazza (1996).

Some studies reported the explanation of this expression. During the act of DSH, many self-harmers described experience of de-realisation and de-personalisation. Such dissociated states are invoked by some psychoanalysis to explain the apparent anaesthesia that allows some self-harmers to not experience pain (Pao, 1969). Episodic increase in opioid activity may explain the clinical observation in many clients who injure themselves – that apparent insensitivity to pain may accompany dissociation (Winchel & Stanley, 1991).

6.5 Repetition of Deliberate Self-Harm

In this study (n=11) 28.2% of DSH clients had a history of repeating acts of DSH from four to ten times. The painful stimulation is demonstrated to result in increased release of endorphins (Willer et al., 1981). Endorphins that are the body's natural painkillers can lead to feelings of euphoria. And in spite of psychological pain, they feel better. Impulse to DSH arises from a craving for endorphins, like any addictive behaviour; over time, most sufferers hurt themselves more often and more severely to achieve the same sense of relief. The presumed positive reinforcement associated with the release of endogenous opiates had been invoked as a possible explanation for the repetitive DSH behaviour that may result in opiate release (Willer et al., 1981).

This study also found that the vast majority (n=33, 84.6%) did not harm themselves in the last month, and this may be because of being under the DTTO service and not being in prison. Because other studies showed that isolation increases aggression; isolation is associated with decrement in serotonin turnover, and this decrement of association with isolation induces aggression (Valzelli, 1967). Imprisonment elicits DSH behaviour because of isolation, which leads to aggression and impulsive acts; however, clients in DTTO service are not isolating, therefore there is less aggression and less impulse for DSH.

6.6 Attention Seeking and Deliberate Self-Harm

Most of DSH acts are done alone, in secret, and without telling anyone (Hawton et al., 2002). They hide their scars. Current study shows this (n=31, 79.5%). This indicates that acts of DSH are not for seeking attention, as another study suggested (Hartman, 1996), although some acts result in an increase of help and others may result in resentment, particularly if they are repeated.

6.7 Management of Deliberate Self-Harm

The result of the study also showed that (n=22) 56.4% of DSH clients never seek any medical treatment for their injury, twenty-five (64%) have never been referred to psychiatrist after DSH, and twenty-three (60%) of the clients felt that they had been ignored or the staff in A&E had been angry with them. These findings highlight important points: people who harm themselves are not recognizing the problem, so they don't seek help; or because they are not popular with health services staff, similar negative attitude is found in the psychiatric services also. They suffer from the stigma of psychiatric problems, and they often are seen as undeserving and detracting from clinical care of others whose illness are not perceived as self-harm (Harris, 2000). There has been a debate as to whether negative attitude towards persons who harm themselves affects the quality of assessment they receive. Dennis et al. (1997) reported that feelings from staff were ranged between indifference, lack of sympathy, anger, helplessness, and anxiety. Surveys of the Emergency Department found that less than half of those admitted to Emergency Department after an act of DSH received any specialist psychological assessment or follow-up (Kapur et al., 1999). And those who received professional help indicated a high rate of dissatisfaction with treatment (Arnold, 1995). These findings are of concern when the risk of repetition is three times higher among those that discharge themselves before an initial assessment is conducted. The responsibility for an adequate risk assessment for not admitting the DSH clients to hospital and/or not being referred to psychiatrists lies with A&E medical staff (Crawford et al., 1998).

Staff of A&E require suitable training and education in the assessment and management of DSH clients (Holdsworth et al., 2001), and improved liaison between the DSH team and psychiatric service is necessary. All of the above may lead to a better outcome in terms of prevention of repetition of DSH. Many of those who injure themselves are strongly aware of the fine line they walk, but they are resentful of mental health professionals who define their incidents of DSH as suicide instead of seeing them as the desperate attempts to release the pain that needs to be released in order to not end up suicidal (Owens & House, 1994).

6.8 Suicide and Deliberate Self-Harm

Suicidal thoughts were common in DSH clients in current study (n=26, 66.7%), and the majority (n=15, 38.5%) reported not being sure if the suicide was associated with the episode of DSH. This indicated the seriousness of the DSH act and the importance of the intervention to save the lives. DSH is considered to be an indicator for future suicide. Analysis of suicide statistics indicates that one among ten persons who self-harm will eventually kill themselves (Kapur et al., 1999). The close link between suicide and DSH emphasises the importance of an adequate psychological assessment for all persons who deliberately harm themselves (Ryan et al., 1996). As instances of DSH increase in intensity and frequency, one can hit a vein or other vital parts, and one can die. Just like entrance drugs may lead to bigger things, the

DSH act will lead to suicide slowly. Focussing attention on this area of practice may enable the target to be achieved of reducing suicide by reducing DSH acts.

6.9 Childhood Sexual Abuse and Deliberate Self-Harm

The vast majority of DSH clients had a past traumatic experience (n=32, 82.1%) mainly because of sexual abuse. Considering the extended amount of literature around the association between childhood sexual abuse and DSH, the coexistence of sexual abuse history was not surprising. Calf (1995) noted that many DSH patients with borderline personality disorder have experienced sadistic sexual abuse from an older person early in life. Subsequent sexual desire, Stone (1998) suggested, is associated with extreme guilt; the self-injury relieves the tension arising out of guilt; the mutilation punishes not only the patient but also the original perpetrator of the abuse. Several authors have observed frequent histories of childhood sexual assault among individuals with DSH, and some have concluded that DSH in these individuals may be the outcome of such abuse (Low et al., 2000). Some research suggests that earlier abuse and more severe abuse leads to more and more severe DSH (Deiter et al., 2000). There is a clear statistical association between sexual abuse in childhood and DSH (cutting, especially on wrist and forearms), as stated by Romans et al. (1995). There is also a complex relationship between childhood abuse (sexual, physical, and emotional abuse) to BPD diagnoses and DSH (Sasone et al., 2002). Although the importance and grave traumatic effects of childhood sexual abuse should not be underestimated, a cause-and-effect relationship between abuse and DSH behaviour should not be automatically assumed. However, sexual abuse may serve to elicit symptoms in an individual already at risk, but frequent histories of such trauma may also reflect a familiar predisposition to impulsive and violent behaviours (Sasone et al., 2002).

6.10 Eating Disorder and Deliberate Self-Harm

A few reported an eating disorder (n=3, 7.7%), and there are many studies indicating the link between the DSH and eating disorder. Eating disorder is an indicator of increased likelihood of substance abuse due to impulsive personality style of eating disorder individuals (Wiederman & Pryor, 1996). The rate of DSH and substance abuse is higher in eating disorder and sexually/physically abused individuals (Dohm et al., 2002). Tobin and Griffing (1996) reported that 80% of eating disorder patients who reported direct DSH acts had been abused sexually.

6.11 Heroin Use in Deliberate Self-Harm Group Versus Other Factors

It was of a particular interest to point out the existence of an underlying factor that is associated with heroin use (as a main factor) in DSH group. Because heroin can be regarded as manifest of self-destructive behaviour, there was a gratuitous finding that heroin users who deliberately self-harm are also nine times more likely to be alcohol users. How alcohol mediates its effect is a topic for further study. It may be the cause or effect of this combination (heroin use and DSH). The fact that statistical analysis didn't demonstrate a strong relationship with other factors (methods of DSH, suicidal ideation, past traumatic history, etc.) might be a result of the small sample. Apparently, this study does not attempt to report any strong relationships. On the opposite side, it just gives an idea of the variables that might be involved in this correlation.

Forensic populations are widely recognised to have high levels of psychiatric disturbances (Fishbein & Reuland, 1994). And this study revealed that.

6.12 The Ethical Dilemma of Deliberate Self-Harm

Clients with a history of DSH were very sensitive to questioning in this matter. However, this is an important risk behaviour which services are increasingly monitoring because of its association with poor outcomes in substance misuse treatment. Every attempt was made to ensure anonymity so that confidentiality during the assessment was maintained. Clients not willing to divulge material of this nature were not pressured to enter the study. Other considerations raised by this research project were the time pressures and general distress to the clients. The reimbursements were helpful in this regard.

Clients who manifested a need for support were offered a referral to see a senior member of the DTTO clinical team for such support, and this was done with the client's consent. There was a small possibility for the confidentiality to be breached for the benefit of the clients. In the event of that situation, the clients were discussed anonymously with Dr Emily Finch and/or Dr Jane Marshall, and an opinion was sought on the best way to move forward.

The finding of this research will enable professionals to develop a better understanding of the issues surrounding DSH among DTTO clients and develop treatment strategies to meet perceived needs. Since DSH is associated with poor outcomes and heavy use of resources in the addiction field, it is important to gain further insight into this behaviour so that services are more aware and proactive. This ultimately has financial and social pay-offs. One study estimated the cost of DSH in the general hospital at around forty-five to fifty million pounds annually. Treatment in intensive care units accounts for less than 10% of hospital costs of DSH (Yeo, 1993).

6.13 Limitations of the Study

The findings of this study will need to be interpreted in light of certain limitations.

First, and perhaps most importantly, caution is needed in generalising the result of this study to the overall substance misuse population for the following reasons: 1) The sample chosen is from the Croydon & LSL DTTO. 2) DTTO clients are in the criminal justice system. 3) The small number of recruits. 4) And the fact that the study is a pilot study.

The way the subjects were recruited may be a limitation in itself. Unavoidably, there were a number of subjects who did not agree to participate. Therefore, even though the recruitment was aimed to be consecutive, those who did not participate biased the sample. In addition, men and women were not recruited in equal number as the sample was predominately male; the number of alcohol recruits were also not equal to the number of drug recruits, and the number of DSH recruits not the same as the number without history of DSH. However, since the aim of this study is not to assess the prevalence of DSH, this study will not be directly affected by the dynamics of the sample. On the other hand, the size of the sample may be affected because the participants may under-report their level of DSH, as this issue is sensitive (*selection bias*). It also should be noted that this study relied on paper-and-pen measured and self-report; responses could be influenced by problems with reading comprehension and concentration. Some caution must be exercised when considering the validity of self-reported data as it is potentially biased because there is always risk of under-reporting owing to imperfect recall (*recall bias*).

The instruments used in this study could also be considered a limitation (*information bias*). The choice of instruments could be questioned since there are a variety of similar instruments that could be used. The selected instruments were chosen to better suit for the purpose of the study, and each one was selected for different reasons. Since there are no standardised criteria or measurements for DSH, the semi-structured self-reported questionnaire was developed to cover all the issues related to DSH. The BDI has been used extensively in other studies for diagnostic purposes. It is well validated and reliable with adequate internal consistency, is easy to use, uses simple language, and is easy to score (Beck et al., 1988). It is useful in this particular study because scores above 40 suggest the possibility of exaggeration of depression, possibly characteristic of histrionic or borderline personality disorder, which are associated with DSH. Significant levels of depression are still possible (Groth-Marnat, 1990).

BIS-11 is a widely known measure of impulsivity and has been valued for its reliability and validity (Barratt & Stanford, 1995). It is used in this study, because it measures impulsiveness in violent patients, substance abusers, and in patients with personality disorders, aggression, suicidal tendency, and other potentially destructive behavioural problems. The two standardised measures of assessment used in this study prevented issues of bias.

7. Conclusion

DSH behaviour is a complex and broad subject, and, at the same time, it is a poorly understood phenomenon. DSH is a symbol of protest, a maker of violation. It is a direct, candid relationship and dialogue with powerful feelings, life circumstances, and extraordinary perceptions. The syndrome is more prevalent than most people think, and yet it is still grossly under-reported and misdiagnosed.

In general, the finding from this study indicates that the preferred substance use (heroin) is the main predictor for DSH. And among heroin users who deliberately self-harm, there is a nine times higher chance to be alcohol users. DSH clients are more impulsive than non-DSH clients. Cutting and overdosing are the most common methods of DSH. The evidence for clear links between substance use, crime, impulsivity, sexual abuse, eating disorder, and DSH is well explored in this study. And it is important that these disorders are identified and treated.

Many professionals continue to define acts of DSH as merely and totally being symptomatic of borderline personality disorder instead of considering that they may well be disorders in their own right. In a society where some individuals think that too many people are using mental disorders as labels or excuses, do we really need yet another mental disorder! In fact, we really don't, but DSH is real. And it appears to be becoming a new trend.

7.1 Recommendations for Future Studies

Townsend et al. (2001) states that 'DSH come from all walks of life and all economic brackets' drawing our attention to the widespread occurrence of DSH across the population. And this is emerging in more recent research on each specific area of DSH. These areas are terminology, causative factors, incidence of DSH in adults and children and different population settings, different cultural settings, current and proposed legislation, and interventions and management of services in terms of class, race, and ethnicity.

Also, further research is required into forms of DSH other than drug overdose, and in particular into cutting, its causes, outcomes and effective treatment.

More recent reports suggest that there are still many questions to be answered in this area.

The risk of repetition of DSH calls for increased efforts to develop interventions that are geared towards the specific needs of individuals; therefore, a larger sample and observation for a longer duration is clearly indicated for future studies. Such studies are much needed, not only because of the dangers associated with the DSH act itself but also because DSH act is a creator of severe social and interpersonal difficulties and psychiatric problems, such as impulsiveness.

The information that draws from this cross-sectional study will have a number of implications for mental health care, research, and training. Among many things, it provides a better understanding of issues surrounding DSH among DTTO clients. This will guide future strategies aimed at increasing access and effective treatment for them.

Finally, this small study can be viewed as an initial attempt to address an issue that has never before been researched in this subject population, indicating the direction that future studies can take. It could include

-Comparison between this sample and a sample from a different geographical location of DTTO.

-Comparison between this study and DSH in the prison population.

-Comparison between this study and DSH in non-drug-using populations.

References

Anderson, M. (1999). Waiting for the harm: deliberate self-harm and suicide in young people; a review of the literature. *Journal of Psychiatry and Mental Health Nursing*, 6, 91–100.

Appleby, L., Morriss, R., Gask, L., Roland, M., et al. (2000). An education intervention for front- line health professional in the assessment and management of suicidal patients. *Psychological Medicine*, 30, 805–812.

Arnold, L. (1995). *Women and self-injury: A Survey of 76 Women*. Bristol: Bristol Crisis Service for Women.

Barratt, E.S. (2003). *Personal communication*. Email: ebarratt@utmb.edu.

Barratt, E.S. and Patton, J.H. (1983). Impulsivity: Cognitive, Behavioural, and psychophysiological correlates. In: M.Zuckerman, Editor, *Biological Basis of Sensation-Seeking, Impulsivity, and Anxiety*. Lawrence Erlbaum Associates, Hillsdale, NJ. p. 77–116.

Barratt, E.S. and Stanford, M.S. (1995). *Impulsivness, in Personality Charactristics of the Personality Disordered Client*. Edited by Costello CG. New York, Wilev. p. 91–118.

Beautrais, AL., Joyce, PR., Mulder, RT., et al. (1996). Prevalence and comorbidity of mental disorders in persons making serious suicide attempts: a case- control study. *American Journal of Psychiatry*, 153, 1009–1014.

Beck, A.T., Steer, R.A., and Garbin, M.G. (1988). Psychometric properties of Beck Depression twenty-five years of evaluation. *Clinical Psychology Review*, 8, 77–100.

Beck, A.T., Ward, C.H., Mendelson, M., Mock, J., and et al. (1961). An inventory for measuring depression. *Archives of General Psychiatry*, 4, 561–571.

Blenkiron, P., House, A. and Milnes, D. (2000). The timing of acts of deliberate self-harm: is there any relation with suicidal intent, mental disorder or psychiatry management? *Journal of Psychosomatic Research*, 49, 3–6.

Boyce, P., Oakley-Browne, M. A. and Hatcher, S. (2001). The problem of Deliberate self-harm. Review Article. *Current opinion psychiatry*, 14, 107–111.

Brady, K.T., Myrick, H., and McElroy, S. (1998). The relationship between substance use disorders, impulse control disorders, and pathological aggression. *The American Journal on Addiction/American Academy of psychiatrists in Alcoholism and addictions*, 7, 221–230.

Brown, M.Z., Comtois, K.A., and Linehan, M.M. (2002). Reasons for Suicide Attempts and Non-suicidal Self-Injury in Women With Borderline Personality Disorder. *Journal of abnormal Psychology*, 111, 198–202.

Calf, D.L. (1995). Chronic self-injury in adult survivors of childhood abuse: Sources, motivations and functions of self-injury (part 1). *Treating Abuse Today*, 5–13, 11–16.

Casillas, A. (2002). Dependency, Impulsivity, and Self-Harm: Traits Hypothesized to understand the associated between Cluster B Personality and Substance use disorders. *Journal of Personality Disorders*, 16, 424–436.

Charlton, J. (1995). Trends and patters in suicide in England and Wales. *International Journal of Epidiomiology*, 24, 45–52.

Conn, L.M., and Lion, J.R. (1983). Self-injury: A review. *Psychiatric Medicine*, 1, 21–23.

Corruble, E., Damy, C., and Guelfi, J.D. (1999). Impusivity: A relevant dimension in depression regarding suicide attempts? *Journal of Affective Disorders*, 53, 211–215.

Crawford, M.J., Turnbull, G. and Wessely, S. (1998). Deliberate self harm assessment by accident and emergency staff--an intervention study. *Journal of Accident & Emergency Medicine*, 15, 18–22

Dear, G.E., Thomson, D.M. and Hills, A.M. (2000). Self-Harm in Prison –Manipulators Can Also Be Suicide attempters. *Criminal Justice and behavior*, 27, 160–175.

Deiter, P., Nicholls, S.S., and Pearlman, L.A. (2000). Self-Injury and Self Capacities: Assisting an Indiviual in Crisis. *Journal of Clinical Psychology*, 9, 1173–1191.

de Moore, G.M. and Robertson, A.R. (1999). Suicide attempts by firearms and by leaping heights: a comparative study of survivors. *American Journal of Psychiatry*, 156, 1425–1431.

Dennis, M., Beach, M., Evans, P.A., Winston, A. et al. (1997). An examination of the accident and emergency management of deliberate self harm. *Journal of Accidence & Emergency Medicine*, 14, 311–314.

Dhossche, D.M., Meloukheia, A.M., and Chakravorty, S. (2000). The Association of suicide Attempts and Comorbid Depression and Substance Abuse in Psychiatric Consultation Patients. *General Hospital Psychiatry*, 22, 281–288.

Dohm, F., Striegel-Moore, R.H., Wilfley, D.E., Pike, K.M. et al. (2002). Self-Harm and substance Use in a Community Sample of Black and White Women with Binge Eating Disorder or Bulimia Nervosa. Periodical, Inc. *International Journal of Eating Disorder*, 32, 389–400.

Dolan, M. (2001). Relationship between 5-HT function and impulsivity and aggression in male offenders with personality disorders. *The British Journal of Psychiatry*, 178, 352–359.

Dunkel, D., Froechlich, S., Antretter, E., and Haring, C. (2002). Replication of two-factor model of Beck Depression Inventory in Alcohol dependence and suicide attempters. *Psychopathology*, 35, 228–233.

Evans, J., Reeves, B., Platt, H., Leibenau, A. et al. (2000). Impulsiveness, serotonin genes and repition of deliberate self-harm (DSH). *Psychological Medicine*, 30, 1327–1334.

Evans, K., Tyrer, P., Catalan, J., Simon, C., et al. (1999). Manual-assisted cognitive-behaviour therapy (MACT): a randomized controlled trail of a brief intervention with bibliotherapy in treatment of recurrent deliberate self-harm. *Psychological Medicine*, 29, 19–25.

Favazza, A.R. (1989). Why Patients Mutilate Themselves, *Hospital and Community Psychiatry*, 40, 137–145.

Favazza, A.R. (1996). *Bodies Under Siege: Self-mutilation and Body Modification in Culture and Psychiatry* (2nd edition). Baltimore, MD: John Hopkins University Press. p. 150–162.

Favazza, A.R. and Conterio, K. (1988). The plight of chronic self-mutilators. *Community Mental Health Journal*, 24, 22–30.

Favazza, A.R. and Rosenthal, R.J. (1993). Diagnostic Issues in Self-mutilation. *Hospital and Community Psychiatry*, 44, 134–140.

Faye, P. (1995). Addictive characteristics of the behavior of self-mutilation. *Journal of* Psychosocial *nursing and Mental health Services*, 33, 36–39.

Fishbein, D.H. and Reuland, M. (1994). Psychological Correlates of Frequency and Type of Drug Use among Jail Inmates. *Addictive behaviour*, 19, 583–598.

Fleming, J., McDonald, D., and Biles, D. (1992). Self-inflicted harm in custody. In D. Biles & D. McDonald (Eds.), *Deaths in custody in Australia 1980–1989: The research papers of the Criminology Unit of the Royal Commission into Aboriginal Deaths in Custody*. Canberra: Australian Institute of Criminology. p. 381–416.

Foster, T., Gillespie, K., and McClelland, R. (1997). Mental disorder and suicide in Northern Ireland. *British Journal of Psychiatry*, 170, 447–452.

Hall, D.J. (1994). A psychiatric Liaison service in a general hospital referrals and their appropriateness. *Scottish Medical Journal*, 39, 141–144.

Harrington, R. (2001). Depression, suicide and deliberate self-harm in adolescence. *British Medical Bulletin*, 57, 47–60.

Harris, J. (2000). Self-Harm: Cutting the Bad out of Me. *Qualitative Health research*, 2, 164–173.

Hartman, D. (1996). Cutting Among Young People in Adolescent Units. *Therapeutic Communities*, 17, 5–17.

Haw, C., Houston, K., Townsend, E. and Hawton, K. (2002). Deliberate self-harm patients with depressive disorders: treatment and outcome. *Journal of* Affective Disorders, 70, 57–65.

Haw, C., Houston, K., Townsend, E., and Hawton, K. (2001). Deliberate Self-Harm Patients with Alcohol Disorders: Characteristics, Treatment, and Outcome. *Crisis*, 22, 93–101.

Hawton, K. (2002). United Kingdom legislation on pack sizes of analgesics: background, rationale, and effects on suicide and deliberate self-harm. *Suicide & Life Threatening Behavior*, 32, 223–229.

Hawton, K., Arensman, E., Townsend, E., Bremner, S., et al. (1998). Deliberate self-harm: systematic review of efficacy of psychosocial and pharmacological treatment in preventing repetition. *British Medical Journal*, 317, 441–447.

Hawton, K., Fagg, J., Simkin, S., Townsend, E. et al. (1997). Trends in deliberate self-harm in Oxford, 1985–1995: Implication for clinical services and the prevention of suicide. *British Journal of Psychiatry*, 171, 556–560.

Hawton, K., Kingsbury, S., Steinhardt, K., James, A. et al. (1999). Repetition of deliberate self-harm by adolescent: the role of psychological factors. *Journal of Adolescence*, 22, 369–378.

Hawton, K., Rodham, K., Evans, E., and Weatherall, R. (2002). Deliberate self-harm in adolescents: self-report survey in schools in England. *British Medical Journal*, 325, 1207–1211.

Heard, H. (2000). Psychotherapeutic approaches to suicidal ideation and behaviour. In: Hawton, K., Van Heerigen, K. (Eds.) *The International Handbook of Suicide and Attempted Suicide*. John Wiley & Sons, Chichester. p. 503–518.

Herpertz, S. (1995). Self-injurious behaviour: Psychopathological and nosological characteristics in subtypes of self-injurers. *Acta Psychiatrica Scandinavica*, 91, 57–68.

Holdsworth, N., Belshaw, D. and Murray, S. (2001). Developing A&E nursing responses to people who deliberately self-harm: the provision and evaluation of a series of reflective workshops. *Journal of Psychiatric and Mental Health Nursing*, 8, 449–458.

House, A., Owens, D., and Storer, D. (1992). Psycho-social intervention following attempted suicide: Is there a case for better services? *International review of Psychiatry*, 4, 15–22.

Gore and Altman. (1982). Statistical in Practice. *British Medical Association. London*. p. 7.

Gossop, M.R., Cobb, J.P. and Connell, P.H. (1975). Self-Destructive Behaviour in Oral and Intravenous Drug- Dependent Groups. *British Journal of Psychiatry*, 126, 266–269.

Groth-Marnat, G. (1990). *The handbook of psychological assessment* (2 ed.). John Wiley & Son. New York. p. 60–65.

Gunnell, D., Bennewith, O., Peters, T.J., Stocks, N. et al. (2002). Do patients who self-harm consult their general practitioner soon after hospital discharge? A cohort study. *Social Psychiatry & Psychiatric Epidemiology*, 37, 599–602.

Kahan, J., and Pattison, M. (1984). Proposal for a distinctive diagnosis: the deliberate self-harm syndrome (DSH). *Suicide Life Threatening Behavior*, 14, 17–35.

Kapur, N. House, A., Creed, F., Feldman, E., et al. (1999). general hospital service for deliberate self-poisoning: an expensive road to nowhere? *Postgraduate Medical Journal*, 75, 599–602

Kreitman, N., and Foster, J. (1991). Construction and selection of predictive scales, with special reference to Parasuicide. *British Journal of Psychiatry*, 159, 185–192.

Illisse, P. (2002). Self-Injurious Behaviors: Assessment and Treatment. *American Academy of Child and Adolescent Psychiatry*, 41, 888–889.

Ireland, J.L. (2000). A descriptive analysis of self-harm reports among a sample of incarcerated adolescent males. *Journal of Adolescence*, 23, 605–613.

Liebling, A. (1993). Suicide attempts in male prisons. *New Law Journal*, May, 649–650.

Linehan, M., Rizvi, S., Shaw Welch, S., and Page, B. (2000). Psychiatric aspect of suicidal behaviour: personality disorders. In: Hawton, K., Van Heerigen, K. (Eds.) *The international Handbook of Suicide and Attemoted Suicide*. Jone Wiley & Sons, Chichester. p. 147–178.

Loucks, N. (1998). HMPI Corton Vale: Research into drugs and alcohol, violence and bullying, suicides and self-injury, and backgrounds of abuse. *Scottish Prison Service Occasional Papers*, 1/98.

Low, G., Jones, D., Macleod, A., Power, M. et al. (2000). Childhood trauma, dissociation and self-harming behaviour: A pilot study. *British Journal of Medical Psychology*, 73, 269–278.

Manfredini, R., Gallerani, M., Caracciolo, S., Tomelli, A. et al. (1994). Circadian variation in attempted suicide by deliberate self-poisoning. *British Medical Journal*, 309, 774–775.

Merrill, J., Milner, G., Owens, J., Vale, A. et al. (1992). Alcohol and attempted suicide. *British Journal of Addiction*, 87, 83–89.

Michel, K., Ballinari, P., Bille-Brahe, U., Crepet, P. et al. (2000). Methods used for parasuicide: results of the WHO/EURO Multicentre study on Parasuicide. *Social Psychiatry and Psychiatric Epidemiology*, 35, 156–163.

Moeller, F.G., Dougherty, D.M., Barratt, E. S., Oderinde, et al. (2002). Increased impulsivity in cocaine dependent subjects independent of antisocial personality disorder and aggression. *Drug and Alcohol Dependence*, 68, 105–111.

Morgan, V., and Coleman, M. (2000). An evaluation of a liaison service in an A&E department. *Journal of Psychiatric and Mental Health Nursing*, 7, 391–397.

Nielsen, D.A., Virkkunen, M., Lappalainen, J., Eggert, M. et al. (1998). A tryptopan hydroxylase gene marker for suicidality and alcoholism. *Archives of General Psychiatry*, 55, 593–602.

O'Connor, R.C., Sheehy, N.P., and O'Connor, D.B. (2000). Fifty cases of general hospital parasuicide. *British Journal of Health Psychology*, 5, 83–95.

O'Sullivan, M., Lawlor, M., Corcoran, P., and Kellehar, MJ. (1999). The cost of hospital care in the year before and after parasuicide. *Crisis*, 20, 178–183.

Owens, D., Horrocks, J., and House, A. (2002). Fatal and non-fatal repetition of self-harm. The *British Journal of Psychiatry*, 181, 193–199.

Owens, D., and House, A. (1994). A general hospital services for deliberates self harm. *Journal of Royal College of Physician of London*, 28, 370–371.

Pao, P.N. (1969). The syndrome of deliberate self-cutting. *British Journal of Medical Psychology*, 42, 195–206.

Patton, J. H., Stanford, M.S., and Barratt, E.S. (1995). Factors Structure of the Barratt Impulsivness Scale. *Journal of Clinical Psychology*, 51, 768–774.

Pembroke, L.R. (2000). Damage Limitation. *Nursing Times*, 96, 34–35.

Powis, B., Strang, J., Griffiths, P., Tylor, C., et al. (1999). Self-reported overdose among injecting drug users in London: extent and nature of the problem. *Addiction*, 94, 471–478.

Romans, S.E., Martin, J.L., Anderson, J.C., Herbison, G.P., et al. (1995). Sexual abuse in childhood and deliberate self-harm. *American Journal of Psychiatry*, 152, 1336–1342.

Roy, A.R., De Jong, J., and Linnoila, M. (1989). Cerebrospinal fluid monoamine metabolites and suicidal behavior in depressed patients. *Archives of general Psychiatry*, 46, 609–612.

Rosen, P.M., and Heard, K.V. (1995). A Method for Reporting Self-Harm According to Level of Injury and Location on the Body. *Suicide and Life-Threatening Behavior*, 3, 381–385.

Ryan, J., Rushdy, A., Perez-Aila, C.A., and Allison, R. (1996). Suicide rate following attendance at an accident and emergency department with deliberate self harm. Journal of *Accident and Emergency Medicine*, 13, 101–104.

Sansone, R.A., Gaither, G. A., and Songer D.A. (2002). Self-Harm Behaviors Across the Life Cycle: A pilot Study of Inpatients With Borderline Personality Disorder. *Comprehensive Psychiatry*, 43, 215–218.

Schalling, D., Asberg, M., Edman, G., and Levander, S. (1984). Impulsivity, nonconformity and sensation seeking as related to biological markers for vulnerability. *Clinical Neuropharmacology* 7 (supp 1), 746–747.

Shaughnessy, J.J., and Zechtmeister, E.B. (1997). *Research Methods in psychology* (4 ed.) New York: Mc Graw-Hill. p. 90.

Shaw, S.N. (2002). Shifting Conversation on Girls' and Women's Self-Injury: An Analysis of the Clinical Literature in Historical Context. *Feminism & Psychology*, 2, 191–219.

Sheard, T., Evans, J., Cash, D. Hicks, J., et al. (2000). A CAT-derived one to three session intervention for repeated deliberate self-harm: a description of the model and initial experience of trainee psychiatrists in using it. *British Journal of Medical Psychology*, 73, 179–196.

Smith, G., Cox, D., and Saradjian, J. (1998). *Women and self-harm*. London: Women's Press.

Solomon, V., and Farrand, J. (1996). Why don't you do it properly? Young women who self-injury. *Journal of Adolescence*, 19, 111–119.

Strong, M. (1998). A bright red scream: *Self-mutilation and language of pain*. New York: Penguin Putnam. p. 62–84.

Suominen, K., Henriksson, M., Soukas, J., Isometsa, E., et al. (1996). mental disorders and comorbidity in attempted suicide. *Acta Psychiatrica Scandinavica*, 94, 234–240.

Tobin, D.L., and Griffing, A.S. (1996). Coping, sexual abuse, and compensatory behavior. *International Journal of Eating Disorder*, 20, 143–148.

Townsend, E., Hawton, K., Harriss, L. Bale, E., et al. (2001). Substance used in deliberate self-poisoning 1985–1997: trends and association with age, gender, repetition and suicide intent. *Social Psychiatry and Psychiatric Epidemiology*, 36, 228–234.

Turnbull, P.J., McSweeney, T., Webster, R., Edmunds, M., et al. (2000). Drug Treatment and Testing Orders: Final Evaluation Report (Home Office Research Study 212) London: *Home Office Research, Development and Statistics Directorate*. Valzelli, L. (1967). Drugs and aggressiveness. *Advance Pharmacology*, 5, 79–108.

Yeo, H.M. (1993). The cost of treatment of deliberate self-harm. *Archive Emergency Medical*, 9, 8–14.

Wiederman, M.W., and Pryor, T. (1996). Substance Use And Impulsive Behaviors Among Adolescents With Eating Disorders. *Addictive Behaviors*, 2, 269–272.

Wilkinson, G., and Smeeton, N. (1987). The repetition of parasucide in Edinburgh 1980–1981. *Social Psychiatry*, 22, 14–19.

Willer, J.C., Dehen, H., and Cambier, J. (1981). Stress induced analgesia in humans. *Science*, 212, 680–691.

Winchel, R. M., and Stanley, M. (1991). Self-Injurious Behavior: A Review of the Behavior and Biology of Self-Mutilation. *American Journal of Psychiatry*, 148, 306–317.

Wylie, K., House, A., Storer, D., Raistrick, D., et al. (1996). Deliberate Self-Harm and Substance Dependence: The Management of Patients Seen in the General Hospital. *The Journal of Mental Health Administration*, 2, 246–252.

Zaidan Z.A., Burke, D.T., Dorvlo, A.S., Al-Naamani, A., et al. (2002). Deliberate self-poisoning in Oman. *Tropical Medical and International Health*, 6, 549–556.

Appendix I

Information and Consent Sheet

History of deliberate self-harm in clients attending the Croydon and Lambeth, Southwark and Lewisham (LSL) Drug Treatment and Testing Orders (DTTO) Services

(Information Sheet and Consent Form)

You are invited to participate in this research project, which study the history of Self-Harm among DTTO clients. Participation involves filling out a self-report questionnaire, which includes questions about you, your use of drugs and alcohol, also whether you have experienced episodes of self-harm or depression.

The findings of this research will enable health care professionals to develop a better understanding of issues surrounding self-harm among DTTO clients, and to develop helpful treatments.

This project is being carried out by Dr Samia Abul, currently studying for a Masters in Addiction at the National Addiction Centre (4 Windsor walk, London SE5 8AF, tel. 020 7848 0823). Dr Jane Marshall, a consultant psychiatrist working at National Alcohol Unit-Alexandra House, is supervising the project together with Dr Emily Finch, the consultant psychiatrist who runs the Croydon and Lambeth, South wark and Lewisham (LSL) DTTO project.

Completion of the attached questionnaire should take approximately thirty minutes. All your answers will be treated in strict confidence, and will be used only for research purposes.

You are free to withdraw from this study at any time. Withdrawal from the study will not affect your treatment in any way.

If you are willing to help me, please sign the consent form in the space provided. I will be pleased to answer any other questions you might have about this.

Thank you for your assistance.

1) I voluntarily agree to take part in the above study.

2) I have been given detailed explanation of the nature and purpose of the study.

3) I understand that I am free to withdraw from the study at any time without having to give a reason. Withdrawal will not affect my treatment in any way.

4) I will not be referred to by name in any report concerning the study. No personal information will be disclosed to any other person not involved in the study.

Volunteer's signature-----------------------------------Date---------------------------------

Volunteer's signature-----------------------------------Date---------------------------------

Appendix II

Questionnaires

History of Deliberate Self-Harm in clients attending the Croydon and Lambeth, Southwark and Lewisham (LSL) Drug Treatment and Testing Orders (DTTO) Services

Date: / /   Serial No._____

I would like you to tick the appropriate answer on this self-report questionnaire or where necessary, write your answer in the space provided, which should take approximately thirty minutes. This information is confidential and will be collected anonymously.

Part One: (Demographic information)

- Age: ☐ Years

- Gender:

  ☐ -Male
  ☐ -Female

- How do you see yourself in term of your ethnic group?

  ☐ -White
  ☐ -Black
  ☐ -Oriental (e.g. Chinese, Japanese)

☐ -Indian/Pakistani
☐ -Other (Please Specify)

- What is your marital status?

☐ -Single
☐ -Married/Cohabiting
☐ -Separated/Divorced
☐ -Widowed

- What is your education level?

How old were you when you left school? ☐
Do you have any qualification?

☐ -Yes
☐ -No

If yes (Please Specify):

☐ -GCSE
☐ -A level
☐ -University
☐ -Other

- What is your employment status?
-

☐ -Employed
☐ -Unemployed

If unemployed, when did you last work? ☐

- What category best describes your home?

☐	-Private home
☐	-Rented home
☐	-Council
☐	-Hostel
☐	-No Fixed Abode
☐	-Other (Please Specify)

- How do you fund your substance use?

☐	-Casual work
☐	-Selling
☐	-Borrowing
☐	-Theft
☐	-Shoplifting
☐	-Other (Please Specify)

- For what reason you are ordered for DTTO?

☐	-Drug supply
☐	-Shoplifting
☐	-Burglary
☐	-Other (Please Specify)

- Length of current DTTO ☐

- Length of previous time in prison ☐

Part Two: (Substance use)

We are interested in finding out about your history of substance use.
Please complete the questions below.

Substance	Ever used	First used at age	Last used	Frequent of using drugs?	Amount consumed in a typical day (£) or the dose	Route (oral, snort, smoke, chase, inject, scripted)
Alcohol						
Heroin						
Cocaine/Crack						
Cannabis						
Benzodiazepines (for example diazepam)						
Other (Please Specify)						

What is your favourite substance among the above?

Part Three: (Self- Harm)

I would like now to ask you some special questions about self-harm.

By this we mean for example: (cutting, overdoing, hurting your body, etc.)

- Have you ever harmed yourself in the past?

☐ -Yes
☐ -No

If yes: How many times in the past? ☐

- How old were you when you first harmed yourself? Years ☐

- Have you self-harmed in the last month? ☐

- Which of the following feelings have you experienced before an episode of self-harm? (You may tick more than one category).

☐ -Emptiness
☐ -Frustration
☐ -Fear
☐ -Agitation
☐ -Anger
☐ -Anxiety
☐ -Emotional pain
☐ -Other (Please Specify)

- What methods of self-harm have you used in the past?

☐ -Cutting (Site of cutting)
☐ -Overdosing (Specify)
☐ -Burning
☐ -Head banging

☐ -Hair pulling
-Picking unhealed wounds
-Other (Please Specify)

- Please tick the category that best describes how you experience pain during an episode of self-harm?

☐ -Severe pain
-Moderate pain
-Mild pain
-No pain

- Please tick the category, which best describes how you feel after an episode of self-harm?
(You may tick more than one, but please note which is the more/most dominant feeling by circling the tick).

☐ -Relaxed
-Euphoric (High)
-Angry
-Regretful
-Other (Please Specify)

For how long does a typical self-harming episode last?

☐ -Less than 5 minutes
-5 to 15 minutes
-15 to 30 minutes
-30 to 60 minutes
-More than 60 minutes

- Many people self-harm while under the influence of alcohol or drugs.
What proportion of your self-harm episodes occur under the influence of alcohol and drugs (%)?

☐ -Less than 20%
-20 to 50%
-50 to 80%
-80% or more

- In your opinion, how do alcohol and drugs affect the episode of self-harm?

-Make worse
-Make better
-No change

- Which of the following provoke episode of self- harm? (Please rate in order of importance):

-Intoxication (Alcohol)
-Intoxication (Drugs)
-Argument
-Feeling low
-Relationship problem
-Nothing much
-Other (Please Specify)

- Have you self-harmed in front of anyone else?

-Yes
-No

- Have you ever sought medical treatment for any of your injuries?

-Yes
-No

- How many times have you attended A&E after an episode of self-harm? [   ]

- How many times have you been admitted to hospital after episode of self-harm? [   ]

- Have you ever been referred to a general psychiatrist for assessment and treatment of your self-harm?

-Yes
-No

- Have you ever been followed up by a general psychiatrist or any member of a liaison psychiatry team? (e.g. Nurse)

	-Yes
	-No

- How do you feel you are treated by staff when you are seen in the A&E department?

	-You are ignored
	-You feel they anger with you
	-You feel they are helpful
	-You feel they are understanding
	-Other (Please Specify)

- Do you want to stop Self-Harming?

	-Yes
	-No

If yes, why? _____

If no, why? _____

- How do you know when to stop self-harming? _____

- Does anything help to prevent you from feeling the need to self-harm?

	-Yes
	-No

If yes, what? _____

- Have you experienced any suicidal ideation in the past?

	-Yes
	-No

If yes, approximately how many times? ☐

- Is suicidal ideation associated with episode of self-harm?

  ☐ -Yes
  ☐ -No
  ☐ -Not sure

- Have you carried out any active suicidal attempts?

  ☐ -Yes
  ☐ -No

If yes, approximately how many times? ☐

If yes, Please describe_____

- Have you had any traumatic past experience (e.g. sexually abused, physically attacked, emotionally neglected)?

  ☐ -Yes
  ☐ -No

If yes, please specify_____

- Do you have any other diagnosed mental illness (e.g. depression, schizophrenia, eating disorder)?

  ☐ -Yes
  ☐ -No

If yes, please specify _____

Thank you for your cooperation.

Appendix III

Beck Depression Inventory (BDI)

Appendix IV

Barratt Impulsiveness Scale (BIS-11)

Appendix V

Receipt for Phone Card Received

Phone Card Received

I have received £5-phone card after filling the questionnaire about 'History of Deliberate Self-Harm in clients attending the Croydon and Lambeth, Southwark and Lewisham (LSL) Drug Treatment And Testing Orders Services'.

Signature----------------------------Date: ----------------------------

I have received £5-phone card after filling the questionnaire about 'History of Deliberate Self-Harm in clients attending the Croydon and Lambeth, Southwark and Lewisham (LSL) Drug Treatment And Testing Orders Services'.

Signature----------------------------Date: ----------------------------

I have received £5-phone card after filling the questionnaire about 'History of Deliberate Self-Harm in clients attending the Croydon and Lambeth, Southwark and Lewisham (LSL) Drug Treatment And Testing Orders Services'.

Signature----------------------------Date: ----------------------------

I have received £5-phone card after filling the questionnaire about 'History of Deliberate Self-Harm in clients attending the Croydon and Lambeth, Southwark and Lewisham (LSL) Drug Treatment And Testing Orders Services'.

Signature----------------------------Date: ----------------------------

I have received £5-phone card after filling the questionnaire about 'History of Deliberate Self-Harm in clients attending the Croydon and Lambeth, Southwark and Lewisham (LSL) Drug Treatment And Testing Orders Services'.

Signature----------------------------Date: ----------------------------

I have received £5-phone card after filling the questionnaire about 'History of Deliberate Self-Harm in clients attending the Croydon and Lambeth, Southwark and Lewisham (LSL) Drug Treatment And Testing Orders Services'.

Signature----------------------------Date: ----------------------------

I have received £5-phone card after filling the questionnaire about 'History of Deliberate Self-Harm in clients attending the Croydon and Lambeth, Southwark and Lewisham (LSL) Drug Treatment And Testing Orders Services'.

Signature----------------------------Date: ----------------------------

Appendix VI

The Ethical Approval Form

Appendix VII

Statistical Analysis

Table 1: Demographic characteristics of consecutive clients attending Croydon and LSL DTTO Service during June and July 2003 (DSH versus no DSH).

Demographic characteristic	DSH (n=39, 100%)	Non-DSH (n=21, 100%)	Total (n=60, 100%)
Gender			
Male	34 (87.2)	19 (90.5)	53 (88.3)
Female	5 (12.8)	2 (9.5)	7 (11.7)
Age			
≤ 35	20 (51.3)	13 (61.9)	33 (55.0)
> 35	19 (48.7)	8 (38.1)	27 (45.0)
Ethnic group			
White	24 (61.5)	14 (66.7)	38 (63.3)
Black	9 (23.1)	6 (28.6)	15 (25.0)
Others	6 (15.4)	1 (4.8)	7 (11.7)
Marital status			
Single	25 (64.1)	15 (71.4)	40 (66.7)
Married/Cohabiting	11 (28.2)	4 (19.1)	15 (25.0)
Separated/divorced	3 (7.7)	2 (9.5)	5 (8.3)
Qualification			
Yes	17 (43.6)	6 (28.6)	23 (38.3)
No	22 (56.4)	15 (71.4)	37 (61.7)

Education level			
No	22 (56.4)	15 (71.4)	37 (61.7)
GCSE	9 (23.1)	2 (9.5)	11 (18.3)
A level	2 (5.1)	1 (4.8)	3 (5.0)
University	3 (7.7)	0 (0.0)	3 (5.0)
Other	3 (7.7)	3 (14.3)	6 (10.0)
Employment			
Employed	3 (7.7)	0 (0.0)	3 (5.0)
Unemployed	36 (92.3)	21 (100.0)	57 (95.0)
Year since last employed			
1–5	7 (17.9)	2 (9.5)	9 (15.0)
6–10	6 (15.4)	2 (9.5)	8 (13.3)
>10	3 (7.7)	2 (9.5)	5 (8.3)
No answer	20 (51.3)	15 (71.4)	35 (58.3)
Employed	3 (7.7)	0 (0.0)	3 (5.0)
Home			
Private	5 (12.8)	3 (14.3)	8 (13.3)
Rented	8 (20.5)	4 (19.1)	12 (20.0)
Council	10 (25.6)	7 (33.3)	17 (28.3)
Hostel	7 (17.9)	4 (19.1)	11 (18.4)
Other	9 (23.1)	3 (14.3)	12 (20.0)

DSH: Deliberate Self-Harm.

Table 2: Relationship between DSH and the demographic characteristic and the reasons, length for DTTO, and length of previous time in prison.

	DSH	Non-DSH	Chi 2	P-value
Gender				
Male	34	19	0.144	1.000
Female	5	2		
Age group				
≤ 35	20	13	0.660	0.590
> 35	19	8		
Ethnic				
White	24	14	0.155	0.783
Other	15	7		
Marital				
Single	28	17	0.611	0.541
With somebody	11	4		
Qualification				
Yes	17	6	1.302	0.282
No	22	15		
Employment				
Yes	3	0	1.700	0.545
No	36	21		
Home				
Rented	8	4	0.4022	0.826
Council	10	7		
Other	21	10		
Reason for current DTTO				
Shoplifting	21	12	0.922	0.395
Other	18	9		
Length of current DTTO (in years)				
1				
>1	19	12	0.728	0.635
	20	9		
Previous time in Prison				
Yes	37	21	1.114	0.537
No	2	0		

DSH: Deliberate Self-Harm.

Table 3: Relationship between DSH and non-DSH and different substance use.

Different substance use	DSH (n= 39)	Non-DSH (n= 21)	Chi 2	P-value
Ever used of alcohol				
Yes	31	13	2.158	0.220
No	8	8		
Age at first use (in years)				
7–12	12	5	1.832	0.279
13–18	19	8		
Not using	8	8		
Ever used of heroin				
Yes	34	16	1.1868	0.298
No	5	5		
Age at first used (in years)				
13–19	15	10	1.305	0.534
20–40	19	6		
Not using	5	5		
Route of administration				
Smoke/Chase	19	11	1.905	0.389
Inject	15	5		
Not using	5	5		
Ever used Cocaine/Crack				
Yes	36	20	0.188	1.000
No	3	1		
Age at first used (in years)				
13–19	15	6	0.587	0.573
20–40	21	14		
Not using	3	1		
Route of administration				
Smoke/Snort	27	15	2.719	0.756
Inject	9	4		
Not using*	3	1		

Ever used Cannabis				
Yes	33	16	0.647	0.493
No	6	5		
Age at first used (in years)				
10–14	21	9	0.659	0.589
15–30	12	7		
Not using	6	5		
Ever used Benzodiazepines				
Yes	17	7	1.302	0.282
No	22	14		
Age at first used (in years)				
13–19	9	4	0.1301	1.000
20–34	8	3		
Not using	22	14		
Ever used of Other substance				
Yes	9	2	1.675	0.299
No	30	19		
Age at first used (in years)				
11–19	6	2	0.760	0.473
20–23	3	0		
Not using	30	19		
Preferred substance use				
Cannabis	1	5		
Crack	9	5		
Heroin	14	9	**11.095**	**0.025**
Crack/Heroin	8	2		
Other	7	0		

*One client from non-DSH did not answer so it was included with not using.

Bold font indicates significant relationship.

df =1, 2, & 4

Table 4: Co-morbidity of DSH and non-DSH with impulsiveness and depression

	DSH (n=39, 100%)	Non-DSH (n=21)	Chi 2	P-value
Impulsivity				
Low	14	4	1.8664	0.365
Moderate	6	10		
High	19	7		
Depression				
Mild	19	7	4.347	0.131
Moderate	10	11		
Sever	10	3		

DSH: Deliberate Self-Harm.

Table 5: Relationship between DSH and non-DSH with impulsiveness and depression

	Odds Ratio	P-value	95% Confidence. Interval
Impulsivity			
Low			
Moderate	1.00	-	-
High	0.344	0.199	0.067–1.754
	0.405	0.223	0.095–1.732
Depression			
Mild			
Moderate	1.00	-	-
Severe	0.350	0.125	0.092–1.340
	1.300	0.796	0.177–9.549

Table 6: Physical pain, typical episode, and the effect of alcohol and drugs on DSH.

DSH	Male (n=34, 100%)	Female (n=5, 100%)	Total (n=39, 100%)
Pain during DSH			
Severe pain	7 (20.6)	1 (20.0)	8 (20.5)
Moderate pain	7 (20.6)	0 (0.0)	7 (18.0)
Mild pain	2 (5.9)	1 (20.0)	3 (7.7)
No pain	13 (38.2)	2 (40.0)	15 (38.5)
No answer	5 (14.7)	1 (20.0)	6 (15.4)
Typical DSH episode (in minutes)			
< 5	13 (38.2)	1 (20.0)	14 (35.9)
5–15	5 (14.7)	2 (40.0)	7 (18.0)
15–30	4 (11.8)	0 (0.0)	4 (10.3)
30–60	3 (8.8)	0 (0.0)	3 (7.7)
>60	2 (5.9)	0 (0.0)	2 (5.1)
No answer	7 (20.6)	2 (40.0)	9 (23.1)
% of DSH under alcohol and drugs			
<20			
20–50	6 (17.6)	2 (40.0)	8 (20.5)
60–80	5 (14.7)	0 (0.0)	5 (12.8)
>80	7 (20.6)	1 (20.0)	8 (20.5)
	16 (47.1)	2 (40.0)	18 (46.2)
Effect of alcohol and drugs			
Make worse	28 (82.4)	3 (20.0)	31 (79.5)
Make better	2 (5.9)	1 (20.0)	3 (7.7)
No change	4 (11.8)	1 (60.0)	5 (12.8)

DSH: Deliberate Self-Harm.

Table 7: History of treatment of DSH of the clients attending Croydon and LSL DTTO Services.

DSH	Male (n=34, 100%)	Female (n=5, 100%)	Total (n=39, 100%)
Medical treatment			
Yes	15 (44.1)	2 (40.0)	17 (43.6)
No	19 (55.9)	3 (60.0)	22 (56.4)
Attended A&E (in times)			
1–2	12 (35.3)	2 (40.0)	14 (35.9)
3–10	5 (14.7)	1 (20.0)	6 (15.4)
Never	17 (50.0)	2 (40.0)	19 (48.7)
Admission to hospital (in times)			
1			
2	8 (23.5)	1 (20.0)	9 (23.1)
3	5 (14.7)	0 (0.0)	5 (12.8)
Never	3 (8.8)	0 (0.0)	3 (7.7)
	18 (52.9)	4 (80.0)	22 (56.4)
Referred to psychiatrist			
Yes	12 (35.3)	2 (40.0)	14 (35.9)
No	22 (64.7)	3 (60.0)	25 (64.1)
Followed up by psychiatrist			
Yes	10 (29.4)	0 (0.0)	10 (25.6)
No	24 (70.6)	5 (100.0)	29 (74.4)
Treatment by the staff in A&E			
Ignored	11 (32.4)	1 (20.0)	12 (30.8)
Angry	8 (23.5)	3 (60.0)	11 (28.2)
Helpful	9 (26.5)	0 (0.0)	9 (23.1)
Understanding	6 (17.7)	1 (20.0)	7 (18.0)

DSH: Deliberate Self-Harm.

Table 8: Different elements in suicide, traumatic experience, and diagnosed mental illness of clients with DSH.

DSH	Male (n=34, 100%)	Female (n=5, 100%)	Total (n=39, 100%)
Suicidal ideation			
Yes	22 (64.7)	4 (80.0)	26 (66.7)
No	12 (35.3)	1 (20.0)	13 (33.3)
Suicide associated with DSH			
Yes	11 (32.4)	1 (20.0)	12 (30.8)
No	6 (17.7)	1 (20.0)	7 (18.0)
Not sure	13 (38.2)	2 (40.0)	15 (38.5)
No answer	4 (11.8)	1 (20.0)	5 (12.8)
Suicidal act			
Yes	17 (50.0)	2 (40.0)	19 (48.7)
No	16 (47.1)	3 (60.0)	19 (48.7)
No answer	1 (2.9)	0 (0.0)	1 (2.6)
Traumatic experience			
Yes	27 (79.4)	5 (100.0)	32 (82.1)
No	7 (20.6)	0 (0.0)	7 (18.0)
Type of traumatic experience			
Sexual abuse	5 (14.7)	4 (80.0)	9 (23.1)
Physical abuse	6 (17.7)	0 (0.0)	6 (15.4)
Mental abuse	7 (20.6)	0 (0.0)	7 (18.0)
Other	9 (26.5)	0 (0.0)	9 (23.1)
No answer	7 (20.6)	1 (20.0)	8 (20.5)
Diagnosed mental illness			
Yes	17 (50.0)	2 (40.0)	19 (48.7)
No	17 (50.0)	3 (60.0)	20(51.3)
Type of diagnosed mental illness			
Depression			
Eating disorder	11 (32.4)	3 (60.0)	14 (35.9)
Other	2 (5.9)	1 (20.0)	3 (7.7)
No answer	1 (2.9)	0 (0.0)	1 (2.6)
	20 (58.8)	1 (20.0)	21(53.9)

DSH: Deliberate Self-Harm.

Table 9: Relationship of heroin use versus other factors in the DSH group.

Variables	Odds Ratio	P-value	95% Confidence Interval
Length of Current DTTO (in years) 1 >1	0.593	0.592	0.088–4.009
Previous time in the prison Yes No	-	-	-
Ever used alcohol Yes No	**8.700**	**0.036**	**1.148–65.932**
Ever used crack/cocaine Yes No	4.000	0.299	0.292–54.715
Ever used cannabis Yes No	-	-	-
Ever used of benzodiazepines Yes No	1.184	0.862	0.175–8.021
Ever used other substance Yes No	0.389	0.348	0.054–2.797
Methods DSH (cutting) Yes No	0.25	0.236	0.025–2.474
Methods of DSH (overdose) Yes No	0.667	0.678	0.099–4.508

Feelings before DSH (emotional pain)			
Yes	3.136	0.245	0.456–21.566
No			
Feelings after DSH (regretful)			
Yes	3.158	0.326	0.319–31.293
No			
Pain during DSH			
Yes	1.586	0.448	0.482–5.221
No			
% of DSH under the effect (alcohol and drugs)			
<50	0.458	0.506	0.046–4.578
≥50			
Medical treatment after DSH			
Yes	0.467	0.435	0.069–3.168
No			
Staff attitude and DSH			
Ignored and angry	2.423	0.366	0.356–16.499
Helpful and understanding			
Suicidal ideation			
Yes	0.458	0.506	0.046–4.578
No			
Traumatic experience (sexual abuse)			
Yes	0.389	0.348	0.054–2.797
No			
Diagnosed mental illness (depression)			
Yes	-	-	-
No			
Diagnosed mental illness (eating disorder)			
Yes	-	-	-
No			

DSH: Deliberate Self-Harm.

DTTO: Drug treatment and Testing Order.

Bold font: significant association.

Deliberate Self-Harm
is a sign of distress not madness
We should be congratulated
on having found a way of surviving

Anonymous

People argue about if it hurts
Some say it does, some say it doesn't
This is my take
If you cut in anger, feeling violence inside, then it hurts
But if you cut with love, if you cut to stay alive
if you cut to relieve all the emotional pain
then the hurt goes away and all that's left is peace

Anonymous

I know what it's
like to want to die
How it hurts to smile
How you try to fit in
but you can't
How you hurt yourself
on the outside to try
to kill the thing on the inside

Anonymous

Anonymous

The great art of life is sensation to feel that we exist, even in pain

Real cutters

don't cut for attention or for the pain

real cutters

cut for the satisfaction

of being in control of something

Anonymous

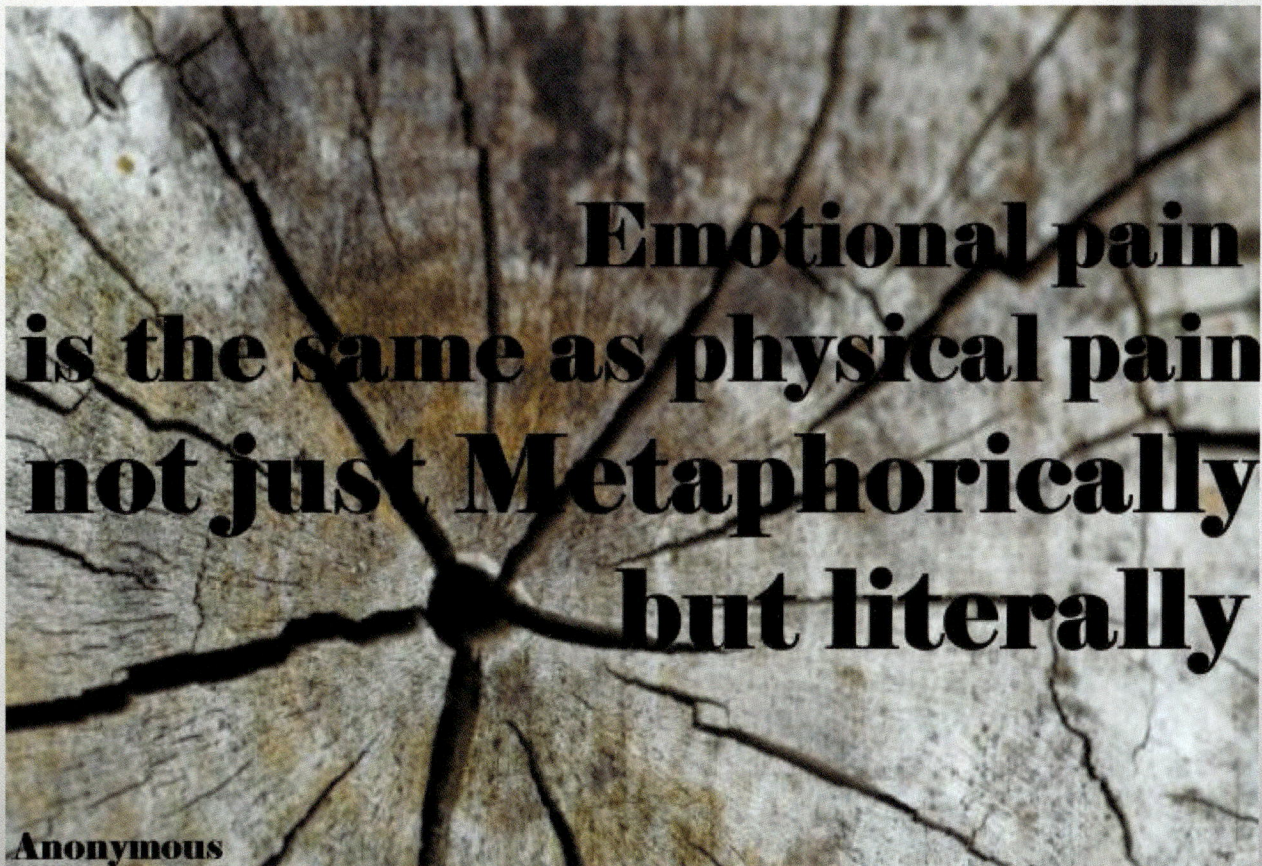

Emotional pain is the same as physical pain not just Metaphorically but literally

Anonymous

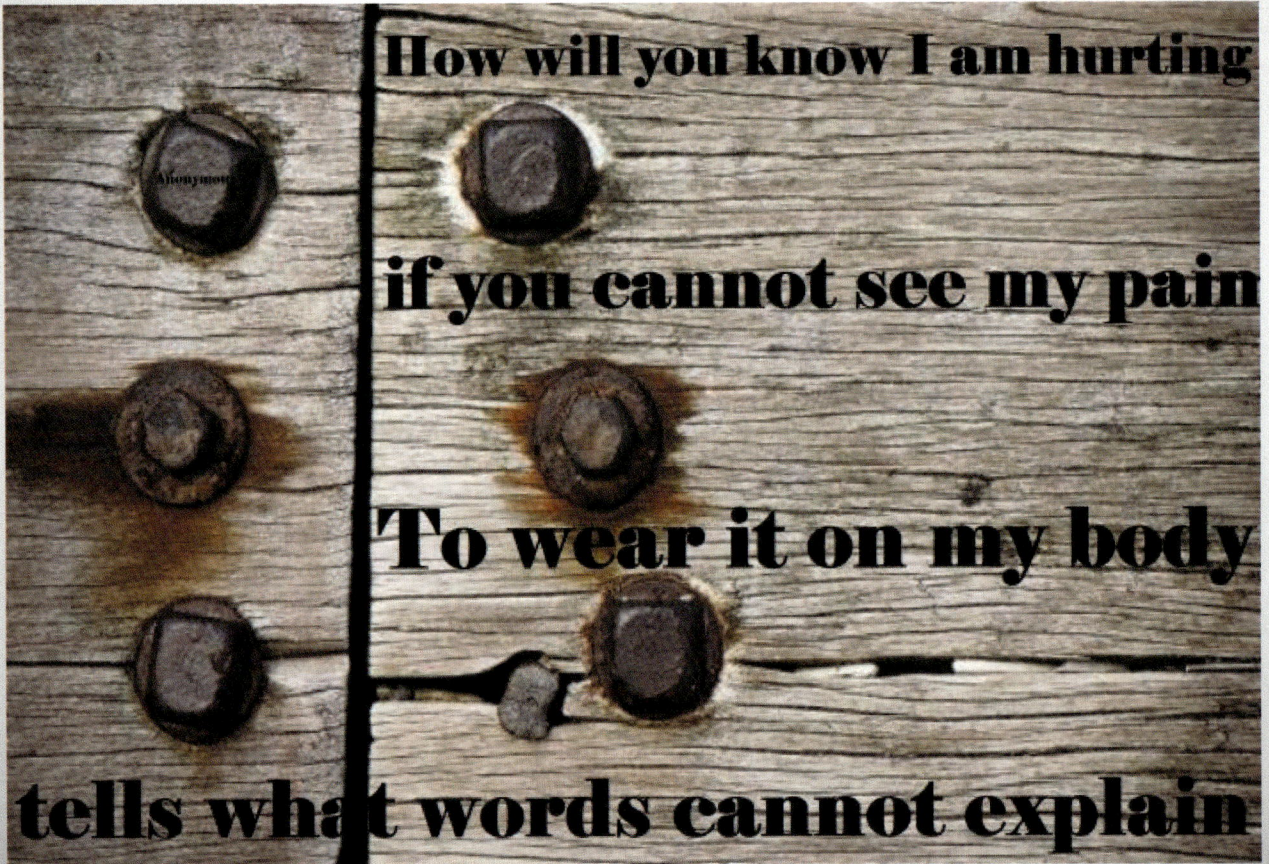

How will you know I am hurting

if you cannot see my pain

To wear it on my body

tells what words cannot explain

The lines I wear around my wrist are there to prove that I exist

Anonymous

I can't stop thinking about hurting myself
Visual bruises can be covered
with make-up, but down to the core
I'm all bruises

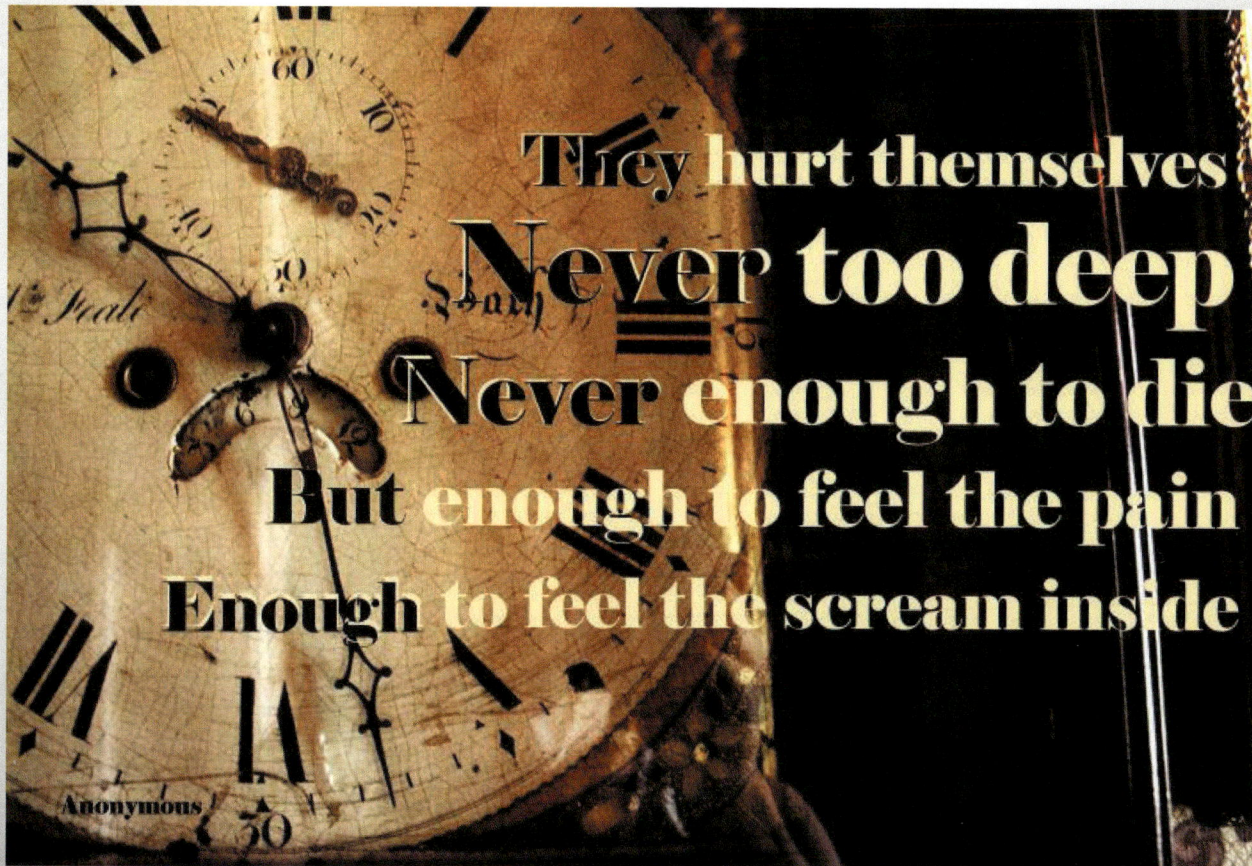

They hurt themselves
Never too deep
Never enough to die
But enough to feel the pain
Enough to feel the scream inside

Anonymous

Index

A

abuse 21, 48, 53
Accident and Emergency Department 23, 43, 51-2
addiction 5, 20-1, 27
addictive behaviour 20, 50
administration 33-4, 38
aggression 18, 49, 51, 56
alcohol 10-12, 15, 17-19, 21, 32, 43, 45-9, 54, 56-7
  abuse 15, 17
  consumption of 10, 32, 46
alcohol users 10, 45-6, 54, 57
anger 19, 52
anhedonia 26
antidepressant 22
antisocial personality disorders 17-18
ASPD (antisocial personality disorder) 18

B

Barratt Impulsiveness Scale 11, 26, 39, 56
BDI (Beck Depression Inventory) 11, 26, 56
Beck Depression Inventory Scale 11, 26
behaviour 5, 13, 18-21, 49, 54-5
  self-destructive 20, 22
  self-harming 22
  self-injurious 16
benzodiazepines 10-11, 36, 38, 45
body tissue 13-14
BPD (borderline personality disorder) 17, 20, 22, 49, 53, 56-7

C

cannabis 10-11, 35, 45
CAT (Cognitive Analytic Therapy) 22-3
childhood 53
clients 5, 10-11, 25-36, 40-5, 47-51, 54-5

cocaine 10-11, 18, 34, 38, 45, 47
confidentiality 54-5
coping mechanisms 21
crime 7, 11, 20, 24, 48, 57
criminal record 21

D

death 13
deliberate self-harm 5, 7, 11, 13-15, 17, 19-23, 27, 31-8, 40, 47-54
delusion 14
demographic information 30
dependence 18
depression 8, 11-12, 18-19, 23-4, 26, 39-40, 42, 45, 48, 56
design 24
disorders
  depressive 18-19
  impulse-control 16-17
drug overdose 14-15, 58
drugs 11, 18, 21, 41, 43, 45, 47-8
DSH (deliberate self-harm) 5, 7-8, 10-15, 17-24, 26-8, 30-58
DTTO (Drug Treatment and Testing Orders) 5-6, 10-12, 23-5, 27, 29, 31, 40-1, 45, 47-9, 51, 55, 58

E

eating disorder 45, 53-4
emotional pain 11, 42, 45, 50
endorphins 50
endorphins theory 21
ethical approval 27
ethnicity 57
excoriation 16

F

failure, past 26
frequency 28, 32-7, 52

R

relationship 8, 10, 23-4, 29, 38-9, 45, 47-8
repetition 22, 52, 58
Repetitive Self-Harm Syndrome 14
research 6, 12, 27, 53, 55, 57-8
risk 20, 22, 52-3, 56, 58
risk factors 19, 21

S

sadness 26
self-abuse 13, 21
self-blame 26
self-dislike 26
self-esteem 22
self-harm 11, 14, 16, 19-20, 44-5, 51-2, 54, 57
  compulsive 16
  episodic 16
  moderate 16
  repetitive 14, 16
self-harm behaviours 16
self-harming 20-1
self-injury 13, 16, 21, 50, 53
self-mutilation 13, 15
self-report 11, 25-6, 56
serotonin 48-9, 51
services, psychiatric 51-2
sexual abuse 45, 53, 57
sexual arousal 14
shoplifting 11, 31
skin-picking 16
statistical analysis 6, 29, 54
substance 5, 10-12, 17-18, 20, 22-6, 28, 31-9, 47-8, 53-7
substance abuse 5, 17-18, 20, 53-4, 56
substance abuse disorders 17-18
substance misuse 11, 23-4
suicidal acts 10, 19, 44
suicidal ideation 18-19, 45, 54
suicidal intent, conscious 13-14
suicidal thoughts 10, 26, 44, 52
suicide 7, 12-14, 19-20, 23, 44, 49, 52-3

suicide rate 19
suicide risk 19

T

tablets 22
therapy 22, 25
  dialectical behaviour 22
tissue damage 13-14
traumatic experience 12, 45
treatment 5, 11, 18, 22-5, 27-8, 31, 43, 49, 51-2, 54-5, 58
  antidepressant 22
trichotillomania 16

V

violence 13

W

women 15, 55
wound 11, 16, 41, 49
wrist 41, 44, 49, 53

CPSIA information can be obtained
at www.ICGtesting.com
Printed in the USA
LVIC06n1704290715
448104LV00016BA/95

9781499086553